Life of a Concubine's Granddaughter

A Baby Boomer's Story

Marie F. Chung

 FriesenPress

One Printers Way
Altona, MB R0G 0B0
Canada

www.friesenpress.com

ISBN
978-1-03-914070-7 (Hardcover)
978-1-03-914069-1 (Paperback)
978-1-03-914071-4 (eBook)

1. SOCIAL SCIENCE, EMIGRATION & IMMIGRATION

Distributed to the trade by The Ingram Book Company

Life of a Concubine's Granddaughter

Preface

I was blessed with my grandmother, porh pawh, which means old woman literally in Chinese. She was my role model, guiding light, and beacon of hope.

This book is dedicated to all the grandmothers who may have a profound impact on their grandchildren in their formative years.

The first wave of baby boomers have been around for three-quarters of a century, surely there is a trove of memories we can share among us. Let me and my fellow baby boomers walk down memory lane and reminisce collectively.

Life of a Concubine's Granddaughter

A Baby Boomer's Story

My life as a concubine's granddaughter began in the fall of 1946 when the first wave of the baby boom started. My maternal grandmother, porh pawh, was born in Guangdong Province, China, at the end of the nineteenth century. She became an orphan when she was a little girl and was adopted by a couple. She was more like a housemaid than a daughter in the adopted family. She was allowed the freedom to play outside with other children in the village. Sometimes she swam in the river nearby. She never went to school. She was illiterate. Her adopted parents intended to marry her off when she was old enough and might make a sizable sum of money from the prospective husband's family. My maternal grandfather, ah kung, himself the son of a concubine, had a wife who was two years older than him. They had six children: two daughters and four sons. His excuse for wanting a concubine was

1

that he did not like his wife's constant nagging. Porh pawh became ah kung's concubine when she was in her early twenties. Ah kung was twenty-seven years her senior. His first-born child with the wife, a daughter, was seven years older than porh pawh. Porh pawh bore eight children: four boys and four girls. My mother was her second-oldest child. One younger daughter and one younger son died when they were small.

I was born in Hong Kong on borrowed time, borrowed and reclaimed land. Hong Kong at that time was a British Crown Colony. I am a British subject by birth. The statue of Queen Victoria sat in the Queen's Square in the central district. China ceded Hong Kong Island to England in 1842, and Kowloon and Stonecutters Island in 1860. In 1898, China leased New Territories with Lantau and surrounding islands for ninety-nine years to Britain and the lease expired on July 1, 1997. Hong Kong Island itself is small and after the Second World War, the population kept on growing. The Hong Kong government expanded the area of the island by way of reclaiming the harbourfront on the northern part of the island.

I was delivered by a midwife. She operated on the second floor of an old low-rise building right beside the Lockhart Road Market in Wanchai. When I grew older and walked by it, I could see that building with a big sign bearing the name in Chinese "No. 5 Big Auntie's Midwifery Clinic" hanging down from the side of the building. There are five children in our family. I am the oldest. Heather was the second-born followed by David and George. Jane is the baby of the family. Heather, David, and George were sub-sequently delivered the same way as I was at the same midwifery clinic. I remembered I went inside the clinic one time when one of my siblings was born there. There were two or three rooms on that floor. I saw a woman lying in a bed in one of the rooms. I did not get to meet the No. 5 Big Auntie who brought me into this world. My mother gave birth to her youngest child, Jane, in a hospital ten years after I was born. At that time, midwifery was probably not a common practice.

Famous people who were born in 1946 are the two former U.S. presidents, George W. Bush and Bill Clinton. According to the Chinese zodiac, 1946 was the year of the dog. So there were two U.S. presidents back to back with dogs as their Chinese zodiac. Barry Gibb of the Bee Gees is several weeks older than me. Tina Fey and Madonna were born in the year of the dog also.

My last name is Chung, which in Cantonese, sounds exactly like Joan. For Chinese, the last names go first. The Hollywood actress Joan Fontaine was well known in Hong Kong at the time I was born, and my father worked in a cinema so he did not have to think to name me Chung Fong Ting.

Ah kung owned an incense stick manufacturing factory near the central district on the island. Most Chinese people worshipped Buddha back in the old days. They burned a lot of these incense sticks in the Buddhist temples or at home. Ah kung's business was thriving. He also owned a masonry shop and a trading company that had business dealings with other countries. He strongly believed that owning real estate was the best kind of investment.

Ah kung and his wife lived with some of their unmarried children in the back part of the third floor above the incense stick factory. Porh pawh and her own children lived in the front part of the same floor. Some of the wife's children occupied the second floor below them. They coexisted peacefully as one big extended family under the same roof when ah kung was around, which was most of the time to keep things under control on the home front.

The wife was blind in one of her eyes due to some eye disease. My mother had to call her *Mother* because she was the legal wife and called her own mother *big sister*. She called ah kung *Dad*.

I called my mother *Mommy*. Mommy went to school until grade 6 when the Second World War broke out. When she was in her early teens, the oldest of her stepsisters was getting married in a village in China. There she met my father, Papa, who was nine years older than her. The bridegroom was the younger brother of Papa's mother. Papa attended a very famous English public high school in Hong Kong. He could speak some English. He smoked cigarettes and Mommy, influenced by him, took up smoking too. When they were back in Hong Kong after the wedding, they went on dates and soon they fell in love. They made a lover's pledge that my father would wait until she was of legal age and then they would get married. When Mommy turned twenty-one years old, she asked porh pawh to get her some suitcases that formed part of her dowry. She would put all her worldly possessions in them and she and Papa would get married.

The thought that Mommy would marry into the family of the wife's son-in-law did not bode well with porh pawh. Porh pawh repeatedly objected to this marriage but to no avail. Finally she gave in to Mommy's relentless pleading.

My parents got married in China where they had moved to during World War II when Hong Kong was occupied by the Japanese. Porh pawh gave Mommy three suitcases and several thousand dollars as her dowry.

On the wedding day, Mommy went over to Papa's house in a buggy with a cover called a *flower buggy* for the occasion of weddings. It was not fitted with wheels but was transported by one man in the front and one man in the back who held onto handles attached to it. When Mommy arrived at Papa's house, a simple wedding ceremony began. She had to kowtow to Papa's parents and his relatives. She offered them tea as part of the custom for brides in Chinese weddings. They had a nice dinner that night. It was a simple celebration. Mommy and Papa finally were married after a prolonged period of dating. She supplemented the household expenses with the dowry money so she could afford to hire a servant.

After the war, my parents moved back to Hong Kong. Papa started working for a good friend of his father, ah ye, my grandfather. Ah ye's friend Uncle Edward owned a Chinese cinema and a house that was a rental property. Papa made a meagre salary working as a bookkeeper in this cinema. Papa rented a storey of Uncle Edward's house, which was near where he worked. This house was situated in the mid-level of a hill in Wanchai. We had to walk one hundred steps up the slope to get to our house. Papa and Mommy lived with ah ye and ah mah, my paternal grandmother. Ah ye also had a concubine. Papa was the first-born. Ah mah gave birth to a girl later. My little ah mah, the concubine, had one son and three daughters. Papa's stepbrother died when he was small. Little ah mah died in her middle age.

We lived on the third floor of the building. There were eight rooms in the flat, one kitchen, one bathroom with a bathtub and a sink, but no toilet. There was a powder room with a toilet and a water faucet with no sink, but a drainage hole on the floor right below it. It was spacious with an area of around two thousand square feet, but we did not have the whole flat to ourselves. Papa sublet three of the rooms on the side facing the Hong Kong harbour to his friend Peter who, with his wife Daisy and their family, occupied two small rooms and one big room with the ensuite bathroom. There were also five children in the family, the oldest, Amy, was three years older than me, and the second child, John, was my age. The rest of their children were around the same ages as all my siblings. Peter's mother lived with them. They also had a live-in maid.

Papa also sublet a bedroom on our side of the flat facing the hill to a newly wedded couple and the servant's room to the groom's parents. By the time I was born, Papa's sister was married and so were two of his stepsisters. We all shared the kitchen and the powder room. We did not have the use of Peter's ensuite bathroom. We had our bath in a big wash basin in the powder room.

An American family of Hispanic descent occupied the floor below us. An old disabled lady lived with her middle-aged unmarried daughter. I never saw the old lady. She stayed indoors all the time. We were often told not to make too much noise or else the old lady would be mad at us. There were two servants working for her. Her two married children came with their families to see her on the weekends.

Just before ah kung died, porh pawh and Mommy's two younger brothers, Uncle Bill and Uncle Bob and her youngest sister, Aunt Betty, moved in with us. Porh pawh, Uncle Bill, and Uncle Bob shared one room, which was originally used for storage. Aunt May was married by that time. We lived on the top floor with a rooftop above it. There was a small room at one corner of the rooftop. Aunt Betty shared this room with Papa's youngest stepsister, Aunt Cecilia.

Ah kung died when he was seventy-four years old. Porh pawh became a widow at forty-seven years old. Buddhists followed a ritual after a person died. Once a week for forty-nine days, they had ceremonies to commemorate the deceased. Buddhist monks would come to the house to pray and chant. Every seven days, immediate family members would take turns to head the ceremonies. On the fifteenth day, it was the turn of the daughters of the deceased to oversee the ritual. When Mommy, Aunt May, and Aunt Betty arrived at their old house, they were refused entry by the wife. They brought along with them incense sticks, candles, and pieces of gold and silver paper denoting valuables the dead people possessed in the afterworld. So they burned all these on the sidewalk in front of the house. They considered this the biggest humiliation of their lives. They talked about it from time to time. Mommy said she would remember it for the rest of her life.

When I was almost three years old, Papa's paternal grandfather died in China, just before it became a communist country in late 1949. Mommy took Heather and me to the funeral. Heather was only a baby born earlier that year. Mommy carried her in a Chinese-style cloth backpack. When we arrived at our great-grandfather's house, we found out that he came back to life. Mommy said that according to Chinese superstition, they believed that it would bring bad luck to the descendants. We stayed behind with our great-grandfather for a few days. I remembered having my dinner in a dimly lit room with the door open overlooking the courtyard. The floor was covered by big red clay tiles. We had steamed egg custard with dried rice grain worms in a big brown ceramic bowl. It was tasty. I also remembered handing my great-grandfather his ceramic bedpan with a handle that was shaped like a flattened kettle.

That is the earliest memory I have of my life. Sometimes I doubted that it might be a figment of my imagination. Years later I checked with Mommy and she confirmed that it was exactly what had happened.

Ah ye's family owned a small building contractor's business. Once a year, all the building contractors celebrated a certain feast day amongst themselves at their firms. It was their custom at dinnertime that on that day they would hand out a bit of food to the children from other neighbouring building contractor's companies. My second-earliest memory of my life is that in the evening of that feast day, our servant took me from company to company in our neighbourhood to look for food. The employees had their feast on the ground floors of the companies with the doors wide open. I remembered our servant and I stood in front of one such company and a man came forward and gave me some food which was called *rice from one hundred households* and it was believed that when children ate it, they would not have to worry about starving all their lives.

My great-grandfather died for real one year later. I did not go to his funeral the second time around. Ah ye died after a while also.

When I was around four years old, Papa bought me a big box of Quality Street chocolate. I ate it all and did not share any with my siblings. It was not a practice for young children to brush their teeth in the morning and at night. Before long, a couple of my baby teeth lost their enamel and turned black.

When I was little, I did not have any toys. I loved dolls. I would carry my pillow in my arms and pretend that it was a doll I was hugging.

Uncle Bob, who was eleven years older than me, liked to fly kites on the rooftop. I watched him and thought it was fun. One afternoon, I used a long piece of sewing thread and attached a square piece of paper to it. I stood on the windowsill in my bedroom and started to fly it like a kite. I got carried away and stepped down on the chair by the window, thinking by doing that it would make the piece of paper fly higher. I missed the chair and fell on the floor and sprained my left arm, which was bent at a right angle at the elbow. Porh pawh knew a woman who was a Chinese-style chiropractor on Spring Garden Street across from Uncle Edward's cinema. She was there only at night. She worked right outside in the middle of the street where street vendors were allowed to set up shops at night when traffic was not allowed. She sat on a stool with an oil lamp beside it. She grabbed my left hand and pulled with all her strength to straighten it. I felt a lot of pain. Porh pawh paid her a small sum of money for her service. Since I was left-handed, I could not hold the chopsticks with that hand, so ah mah spoon-fed me for a while.

Ah mah's feet were called *three-inch golden lotus*, which meant bound feet achieved when girls were very small. It was a status symbol in the old days in China. Since porh pawh was only an adopted child, she did not have bound feet. Ah mah seemed to have a chip on her shoulder. As far as I could remember, I heard her complaining constantly. She was mad at us children all day long. Nothing we did could ever please her. Even though she was not a smoker, she had a chronic cough that lingered on for years. Mommy felt very uncomfortable about that. She was afraid that it might be contagious.

When it was time for me to go to kindergarten, Mommy asked porh pawh to take me to a school in the vicinity to enrol me. It was an all-day kindergarten. At lunchtime, Mommy came and took me home for lunch. One afternoon, Mommy was busy so she asked Uncle Bill to drop off lunch for me. I ate all the six buns he brought me. Papa did not know that Mommy had already sent Uncle Bill over. He came too with six cupcakes and a roll of candies. I felt bad when I noticed that the classmates around me watched with envy while I was devouring the cakes, so I shared the candies with them.

After a year in kindergarten, Mommy wanted me to attend grade 1 at a nice Catholic girls' school. I had to write an entrance examination before I could be accepted into the school. Aunt Betty went with me the morning of the examination. By that time, the money Mommy got as part of her dowry had dwindled and with Papa's low income she could not afford to feed us three meals every day. When I sat at the desk to write the examination, I felt dizzy because I did not have breakfast that morning. I rested my head on my folded hands on the desk until Aunt Betty came to take me home. That school year, Mommy sent me to evening classes for three hours a night. The school was by the harbourfront. David went to that same school during the day. Mommy took him to and from school, but she did not do the same for me. I was only six years old and I walked unaccompanied on the streets during evening rush hours. Mommy never taught me to look both ways before I crossed the street. I had to cross several main streets with heavy traffic. Traffic lights were not installed at many of the intersections at that time. I remembered one evening as I was trying to cross the street on the way home, I saw a red sports car racing close by, but I dashed across the street anyway and was lucky I was not struck by it.

After one year attending evening classes, I was admitted to an Italian convent school for girls. I enrolled in grade 1. All the subjects were taught in Chinese except one English literature course. I had to wear a uniform to school, a white cotton dress in the summer, a navy blue woollen pleated dress and a navy blue woollen jacket in the winter. Mommy made the dress for my winter uniform with man-made fabric because woollen material was much more expensive. For the first winter at school, Mommy could not afford to buy me the jacket. She made me wear Uncle Bob's old black jacket instead. I felt ashamed of myself being the only student in the whole school wearing a different coloured jacket. I never owned a pair of gloves. With temperatures hovering around 10 degrees Fahrenheit in winter, it would have been nice if we could have put on gloves to keep our hands warm.

It rained very often during the typhoon seasons. When I was in grade 4, I got a vinyl see-through raincoat. Since vinyl material is not durable, soon the raincoat ripped and I did not get a replacement all through the rest of my years in school. I had umbrellas but not rain boots.

I did not like school. My attention span in class was short probably due to the fact that I was malnourished. Most mornings I went to school without breakfast. A child cannot learn on an empty stomach. I experienced hunger first-hand. I did not do well at school at all. What I liked was to play with my classmates in the schoolyard during recess. I ran a lot and fell often and skinned my knees. One winter, Mommy bought me white cotton tights to wear to school. Before too long, I made holes in the tights when I ran and fell. Mommy never got me another pair. I also liked to skip ropes. They were readily available at a low cost. We later made skipping ropes out of elastic bands by hooking them up, one by one, to our desired length.

My classmates and I sometimes played a rope game that involved four participants. Two of us on opposite ends were swinging the rope up and down while the other two, "Peter and Paul," were skipping together and all of us were singing, "There are two blackbirds sitting on the wall. One named Peter. One named Paul. Fly away, Peter. Fly away, Paul." Peter and Paul skipped away from the rope respectively.

A very wealthy Chinese family lived right across the street from us in a huge mansion. Around the mid-1950s they decided to build a driveway leading to the main entrance to the house. For some reason, the construction trucks delivering the building materials did not come right up to the front of the house. One late afternoon while I was looking out of my bedroom window, I saw a construction worker carrying a bundle of at least ten-foot-long steel rods on his shoulder, walking up the one hundred steps leading to the mid-level where the mansion was. He was almost at the top of the stairs when suddenly I witnessed the bundle of steel rods slip out of his hands. Following a short distance behind was a young lady who was the daughter of one of the housemaids working in the mansion. Her daughter was an office worker and was on her way home from work. She was allowed to stay with her mother in the servant's quarters. The steel rods fell on her face and miraculously she escaped serious injury.

On the completion of the driveway, the owner of the mansion threw a lavish party to mark the occasion. All the who's who in Hong Kong were invited. Their chauffeur-driven luxurious cars such as Rolls-Royce, Mercedes-Benz, Jaguar, etc., pulled up to the newly completed driveway. Mommy often said to us, "You kids did not know where to choose a home to be born. If you crossed the street at the time of your birth, you would be born into a wealthy family." In a way, living in the shadow of the filthy rich, I did not feel that poor. There was a sort of rubbing-off effect on me. I had a glimpse of how rich people lived from the outside looking in.

In the 1950s, radio was possibly the only home entertainment unit in most of the homes in Hong Kong. Television was not common yet. In my bedroom there was a small, antiquated tabletop radio with a rotary plate for changing radio stations. Ah mah, porh pawh, and I were glued to it to listen to the daily Chinese soap operas, Cantonese songs, and Cantonese operas about ancient Chinese histories or stories of the olden days. There were live broadcasts of these Cantonese operas especially around Chinese New Year. After a while, the radio stopped working when the rotary plate got stuck. I put my tiny hand inside it to make the plate turn and fixed it. I did not want to forgo my only source of home entertainment. We could not afford to buy a new one.

Porh pawh loved to watch Cantonese operas. She had a favourite male opera performer whose famous role was playing the part of the love monk. He was handsome and had a good voice. When he performed in the Go Sing theatre near the central district, porh pawh went with me to the show. There were three levels in that theatre. The cheapest ticket price with no assigned seats was available on the third level. Porh pawh liked to go to the opening night of each opera. She left with me as soon as I came home from school at three thirty in the afternoon to head to the theatre. We were always the first ones to arrive in the theatre to assure we had front-row seats. At around dinnertime, Mommy came to drop off food for us.

On the opening night, the show started earlier because there was a pre-show act involving the ceremony for the newly appointed ancient Chinese six nations' prime minister. The female lead opera performer drove the prime minister in a symbolic cart. This act was supposed to be for the ghosts of the theatre so they would leave the actual show alone. In one opera at another theatre, they cancelled the pre-show on opening night because the show, which was about ghosts, was very long. During the performance, a very famous songwriter, who wrote the songs for that opera, died while watching his own work in the theatre. It could not be explained whether it was a sheer coincidence or superstition.

After each opera, porh pawh and I had to take the bus home. The last bus was around 12:30 a.m. When the show was just about to end, porh pawh and I left the theatre and ran for the bus.

Porh pawh sometimes went with me to see Chinese movies. One night we went to see two movies, one at 7:30 p.m. and the other one at 9:30 p.m. The theatres were several blocks from one another. After the 7:30 p.m. show, we ran to the other theatre for the 9:30 p.m. show.

Porh pawh was fun-loving and was ahead of her time. She had a free spirit. She lived life to the fullest. She instilled some of her zest for life, energy, and positive attitude in me. She was the driving force behind me and I was motivated by her.

Porh pawh inherited three properties from ah kung on his death. They were not situated in prime locations. One was a three-storey rental apartment building on a dead-end street in the western part of Hong Kong Island. The other two were older houses in Ap Lei Chau, a small island across from Aberdeen on the southwestern part of Hong Kong Island. The renowned Tai Pak Floating Seafood Restaurant was situated in between these two islands. Hollywood movie stars who came to Hong Kong liked to dine at that restaurant. They had their photos taken to line the wall inside the restaurant.

Porh pawh lived on the rents she collected from the tenants every month. Aunt Betty and Uncle Bob were in their teens when ah kung died. They still went to school. Uncle Bill was unemployed. He spent a good part of the day sleeping. He hardly went out. Porh pawh had to be careful utilizing the rent money. Occasionally she took me along to collect rents. One of the tenants in the apartment building was a middle-aged man who was a street-food vendor. He did not always pay his rent on time and he was rude to her.

Porh pawh had to hire a sampan to go to and from Ap Lei Chau every month. We sat near the back part of the sampan and a woman stood in the front to paddle it as it inched ever so slowly towards shore. The two houses there were commercial properties which consisted of a grocery store in each of them. These were single-storey houses. Now Ap Lei Chau is connected to the Hong Kong Island at Aberdeen by a bridge and is well developed with high-rise apartment buildings.

Aunt Betty started dating in her late teens. Her boyfriend, Norman, was a bus driver. His parents died when he was a young boy and he and his younger sister then lived with their mother's older sister. He did not have the chance to go to school. He worked in a British army barrack when Hong Kong was occupied by the Japanese during the Second World War. There he befriended a British soldier who taught him English and driving. He first noticed Aunt Betty when she got off the bus after school. He was attracted by her beauty and youth. He waited at the bus stop for her every day. Finally he came forward and introduced himself to her. Porh pawh did not like him at all, but there was nothing she could do to break them up. My siblings and I did not like him either. He had a fierce look in his eyes. I did not feel comfortable around him. He was on the chubby side so we nicknamed him "fat man."

After years of dating, porh pawh had to accept him and let him come for visits. He tried hard to please her. One weekend he took Aunt Betty, porh pawh, and me to Macau, the Las Vegas of the Orient. There was no hydrofoil going between Hong Kong and Macau at that time. We went on a big ferry which took hours one way. We left home late Saturday night and arrived in Macau early Sunday morning and went back to Hong Kong late Sunday night so we did not need to stay in a hotel. Before we left Macau Sunday night, we saw a Chinese movie called *Nine-Fingered Monster*. I watched the scary scenes through the slits of my fingers placed over my eyes.

We spent the night on the ferry to get back to Hong Kong. No tickets were required for young children when accompanied by adult passengers. Porh pawh slept on a canvas chair and I slept on the wooden floor at her feet. I woke up with a stiff neck that Monday morning.

I was six years old when Queen Elizabeth II succeeded to the throne. There were events to mark the occasion in Hong Kong. Schoolchildren were given red or pink plastic cups with silver-plated cupholders as souvenirs. At night there were fireworks over the Hong Kong harbour. The coronation was filmed in black and white and was later shown in an iconic theatre on Hong Kong Island. Porh pawh got tickets for the show for the two of us.

At that time there were no washing machines or dryers. People washed their clothes by hand and then hung their wet clothes on long bamboo sticks supported on each end by horizontal wooden poles sticking out the windows from apartment units. While we were walking past an apartment building on the way to the show, a bamboo stick fell vertically from above and landed on porh pawh's shoulder. Fortunately it missed the top of her head just by a matter of inches, so she did not sustain a life-threatening injury. Porh pawh was mad and feisty. She looked up and shouted at the woman who dropped the stick. She decided to report the incident to the police. She took me home first to ask Aunt Cecilia to go to the show with me in her place. I remembered the scene when Queen Elizabeth II was being crowned.

When ah kung was still alive, there was a young live-in maid, Ah Hope, working for the family. When she was old enough, she got married to an older man who owned a small store on Third Street just below the mid-level in the west part of Hong Kong Island. He repaired small metal cooking utensils. Porh pawh took me to see them during Chinese New Year. They lived at the back part of the store. Ah Hope's husband was very hard-working. On every one of these yearly visits, I saw him hammering away on the dented aluminum saucepans the whole day. Before dinner, Ah Hope, porh pawh, and I went to the market nearby to shop for food for dinner that night. As it was wintertime, we always had hotpot, which would keep us warm. Ah Hope bought vegetables, meat, seafood, and goose intestines, and we each cooked what we liked with our chopsticks in the rolling hot water. I had not heard of foie gras yet, but the goose intestine was a delicacy to me. We ate at a table on the sidewalk in front of the store. Ah Hope and her husband had a daughter in her early twenties and they adopted a young boy. On one of these visits, Ah Hope's daughter took me to a park at the mid-level. She bought an ice cream sandwich. After a few mouthfuls, she let me have a bite. It was the first time I ever had that and it was yummy. Ah Hope's daughter got married that year. She gave birth to a baby girl a year later but died shortly after giving birth. Ah Hope took the baby home and assumed the role of mother to her granddaughter. Porh pawh and I stopped going to Ah Hope's home from then on.

On some cold winter days, porh pawh went with me to the western district where stores kept snakes in cages. Porh pawh asked for a snake bile drink that could keep her warm. The store-keeper pulled a snake out of the cage and went to the back of the store to prepare it. He came out with a small cup containing the dark greenish bile. Porh pawh gulped it down. They then made soup with the snake meat at some restaurants. I had it and found it tasty.

Aunt May got married in the late 1940s. Her husband, Uncle Simon, was a widower with no children. He was five years older than she was. They had a son, Christopher, who is a few months younger than Heather. They also had a daughter, Rose, who is around six months younger than David. They lived in a public housing apartment building in Kowloon. There were ten units on each floor. Their unit consisted of one room where they ate and slept. There was a balcony, a small kitchen, and an enclosed toilet with no bathroom. They had their bath in a wash basin in the kitchen. Once a month, pawh porh and I went to visit them on the weekends. We usually left home on Saturday nights. We stayed there overnight, sharing the same room with everybody. There was one double bed and one bunk bed. Porh pawh and I slept on the lower bunk bed. On Sundays, we went to the nearby market to shop for groceries. Occasionally we went to a matinee Chinese movie at the cinema near the market. Sometimes I played with my cousins outside the apartment building. We had dinner early Sunday evenings before returning home.

On a few occasions when school was out for the summer, I stayed behind longer by myself with Aunt May and her family. One time Uncle Simon and Aunt May took my cousins and me to a movie called *Old Yeller*. After the movie we ate at a Chinese restaurant. It was a delicious dinner, which left a lasting impression on me. The last of such stays with them during the summer holidays ended when I was nine years old. A boil developed on the bottom part of my back soon after I arrived at their apartment. It got worse in a few days. My body was bent almost in half. I went home immediately. After a few days it did not get better. Mommy took me to a Chinese medicine doctor. His office was on the second floor in the central district. Since I could not climb up the stairs in my condition, Mommy had to carry me on her back. She could not possibly ask porh pawh to take me there because she was too old to give me a piggyback ride. After I was on the bitter herbal medicinal tea for a few days, the boil shrank and I could stand straight again.

At this point in my life, Mommy had hardly ever done anything with me. She did not pay much attention to me. As far as I was concerned, porh pawh was my grandmother and mother all in one. Although Mommy was the one who gave birth to me, I did not consider her my mother.

Porh pawh loved walking. On most weekends, she took me along to walk up from our house on the second level to the third level. Near the top of the slope it was like going up a ladder and on the way down it was a steep descent. Higher up the third level there is a rock shaped like a human being. People believed that it would help single people to find their mates. On certain days of every month, worshippers would go before this rock to burn incense sticks or candles and pray that their wishes would be granted. Since Uncle Bill and Uncle Bob had no girlfriends yet, porh pawh sometimes went up with me to implore its intervention.

Once in a while, porh pawh was very ambitious and went with me all the way up the fourth level, which is the Bowen Road. Sometimes after our morning walk, porh pawh and I went to the bustling open market on the first level. There were roadside vendors selling congee, Chinese doughnuts, and rice rolls. We bought breakfast from them and ate at the table nearby in the open air.

Sometimes in the evening, porh pawh and I went for leisurely strolls around our house. In the summer we walked to the harbourfront at the Wanchai Ferry Terminal. If we went before dinner, we could buy live fish from the fishermen selling their catch of the day from their boats. There was a man at the waterfront selling ice cream in a tricycle. Sometimes porh pawh bought mango ice cream in a cup from him. Although she did not eat beef or any dairy products, she loved mango ice cream.

On some Saturday afternoons, porh pawh took me to the Hong Kong Jockey Club in Happy Valley. We were admitted free of charge as spectators into the grassy ground in the centre, bound all around by the racetrack. Porh pawh never bet on horses. She just loved the action and excitement. Between races I walked on the ground alongside the length of the track until I dropped. My feet were sore later that night.

Porh pawh was a devout follower of Buddhism. She prayed while holding the rope of Buddhist beads every morning. She worshipped in the Buddhist temples regularly. Sometimes I accompanied her. She liked to go to the Female Buddha Temple, which is just east of the Man Mo Temple, one of the tourist attractions. It is situated right at the top of a flight of long stairs. I waited outside for her. There were many street vendors around that area. It was lunchtime one afternoon when I saw a female street vendor getting ready for lunch. She put a pot of rice, a plate of food, and a pot of hot water on the step in the middle of the staircase. She gathered three or four of her children around her and started eating.

Once a year, porh pawh went with me to a temple called Wong Tai Sin who was known as the Great Immortal Wong. His worshippers believed he had answered many prayers. Some good professional soccer players in Hong Kong were nicknamed Wong Tai Sin. In Cantonese, the words *pray* and *ball* sound the same. When the ball player shot and scored, it could be taken as the prayer was answered.

Aunt Betty and Norman sometimes took me along on their movie dates. A child under a certain age accompanied by an adult could be admitted into the cinema for free. I sat with Aunt Betty at one of the front corners of her seat. We watched Doris Day's *The Man Who Knew Too Much*. Afterwards, they kept playing the song "Que Sera, Sera" sung by Doris Day in the movie on the radio. We watched another Doris Day movie *Pillow Talk*. Rock Hudson was the leading actor. Some other movies we watched included *Houseboat* starring Sophia Loren and Cary Grant, and *Imitation of Life* with Lana Turner and John Gaven in it. Lana Turner's daughter was in the news at the time, or soon after that movie was in the theatre. It had something to do with the law. We watched Kim Novak in *Picnic*, James Stewart in *Rear Window*, and Anthony Perkins and Janet Leigh in *Psycho*. I liked an actor with a baby face. I wished my future boyfriend had a baby face, but I was sure no boy with a baby face in his right mind would lay an eye on me.

One Sunday morning, before Aunt Betty went out to meet Norman, she said that she and Norman would take me to a movie that night. I polished my shoes to wear to the movie. As the evening approached, I kept looking out from the balcony outside my bedroom to watch for Aunt Betty and Norman to come home. Finally they showed up, but said they had changed their mind not to go out. I was very disappointed after waiting all day.

Our house was located in a quiet neighbourhood. We would not go out alone at night if we did not have to, especially at the time of the kidnapping of a rich man's grown-up son. There were three kidnappers who were dubbed *the three wolves*. The hostage was eventually killed.

Aunt Betty went to an American convent school. When I was five or six years old, Aunt Betty took me to Sunday school there. It was in the central district. After we got off the bus on Queen's Road Central, Aunt Betty let me have congee at the food stall by the bus stop. She stood behind me to watch me eat before we went to her school.

On hot summer days, I went to Sunday school wearing sundresses with matching short-sleeve jackets sewn by Mommy. There were two other girls my age in the class. After class one Sunday, our teacher, the American nun, Sister Margaret, said to Aunt Betty that the three of us took turns to put our hands over our mouths to yawn during class. That was probably because we got up early in the morning to get ready.

When I was around eight years old, Mommy, Aunt Betty, Heather, David, George, and I converted to Catholicism. Soon after, ah mah, who worshipped Buddha as almost all of the older Chinese people did at that time, became a Catholic also. She reasoned that the Catholic cemetery in Happy Valley was close to our house. After she died, she would be buried there and we could go more often to pay her our respect in her grave.

For several years, our parish church was supplied with bags of flour and rice and blocks of cheddar cheese, which were donations from some American charitable organization to be distributed to the needy parishioners. Mommy and I went to line up for the foodstuff. I never had any cheese in my life until then. Mommy used the flour to make handmade noodles. Ah mah went too on a rickshaw to get her share. Since she had bound feet, she walked at a snail's pace with a walking cane and she had motion sickness riding on motor vehicles, so a rickshaw was her only means of transportation. It took her a long time to walk to mass every Sunday.

I did not do well at all when I was in primary school. One year Mommy decided that I needed tutoring after school. She asked porh pawh to take me to the tutor whom Peter and Daisy sent John, their son, to. Instead, porh pawh took me to the one next door. He was not as good and was not much help to me.

When I was in grade 4, my English teacher did not like me writing with my left hand.

She made me write with my right hand until I was used to it. I can never in my life use scissors and sharp knives with my right hand though.

Jane, my youngest sibling, was born when I was ten years old. According to Chinese custom, when the baby is one month old, the mother would give slabs of barbecued pork and eggs dyed red to relatives. On the day Jane turned one month old, I went with Heather to deliver such stuff to Aunt May's family. It was the first time for me, a ten-year-old girl, to take my eight-year-old younger sister with me to take the ferry and the bus to go all the way to Aunt May's house in Kowloon and found our way back home safe and sound.

One weekend, porh pawh went with me to stay with Aunt May. Jane was about one-year-old and she was sick with fever while we were away. When we got back home that Sunday night, Norman was at our house and he lectured me on my spending the weekend away from home when I should be around helping to take care of Jane. I did not like what he said and thought it was none of his business.

One night, Peter and Daisy took their children and me to a movie starring Charlie Chaplin called *The Kid*. Jane, who was two years old at that time, had the same look and hairstyle as the kid in the movie. I said to myself that when I got home, I would go and take a look at Jane even though she must be sleeping.

When I was around ten or eleven years old, I became aware that I had buckteeth and there was a gap between my right front tooth and the one beside it. At the same time, Mommy said that my eyeballs were bulging and the front of my neck around my throat was swollen, which might be a symptom of goitre. I found that disturbing, especially coming from my own mother. This made me very self-conscious and sensitive. That gave me the impression that I was an ugly duckling. She did not know that "If you don't have something nice to say to anybody, don't say anything." The more I thought about it, the more I realized that beauty is skin-deep. It is what is inside that counts. From then on, I never looked at people the same way. I did not judge them anymore by their look or appearance, but by the kind of person they were.

In the late 1950s, my parents' relationship became strained. Papa had a drinking problem. He drank cheap rice wine sold in bulk at the grocery stores. That was all he could afford. It cost one dollar per bottle. Sometimes he sent me to get the wine for him for lunch. The wine was in a big earthen container. The store clerk poured it into a half-litre glass bottle with a ladle. Then he wrapped the bottle with old newspaper so as not to show the content. While I was walking home, I knew the pedestrians could tell what I was holding in my hand. I felt ashamed of what I was carrying. Sometimes on my way home in the middle of the day, four women, one or two of them with babies on their laps, were playing mah-jong at the foot of the slope right outside their apartment building.

When I was old enough to get an allowance, Papa told Mommy to give me $3 every month. I put the money in the side pocket of ah mah's leather suitcase in our bedroom. I seldom spent any of it. Sometimes when Papa did not have money for the wine, he asked me to give him back $1. When he got drunk he became a different person. He was mean and nasty to us children. He was like Dr. Jekyll and Mr. Hyde. He lagged behind in handing over his monthly earnings to Mommy more frequently. He made $400 per month, which was not much for a big family like ours. Whenever he did not hand over his pay to Mommy in time, she yelled and shouted at him when he came home at midnight after the last show at the cinema. She was a shrew. Papa did not give in to her. They would carry on the shouting match for a long time. This woke up everybody in our flat. After ah mah, Heather, and I were woken up, we sat on the bed we shared together. When Papa finally gave his pay to Mommy she bought meat for dinners. We had live chickens only for special occasions like Chinese New Year. Mommy did not eat beef. She cooked it for us sometimes, but I was allergic to it anyway. I was also allergic to shellfish when I was young.

At the end of the month, most of the money ran out, Mommy made unpalatable meals, which I had no appetite for. She cooked cabbages with dried bean thread and dried shrimp. She bought the cheapest red striped fish for protein. Once in a while I heard on the news that people suffered food poisoning from eating that kind of fish, and I wished Mommy had heard that too and stopped buying it because I hated it.

After Aunt Betty graduated from high school near the end of the 1950s, she worked as a store clerk for a while, then she became a teacher. Sometimes after she got paid, she bought us loaves of white bread and margarine as an after-school snack.

One hot summer afternoon, Aunt Betty and Norman came home with a big carton of Neapolitan ice cream. It was an unexpected and pleasant treat.

On one of Aunt Betty's birthdays, Norman gave her a birthday cake decorated with tiny edible silver beads. I had a big piece but

I did not feel well while eating it. The next morning I came down with the flu and could not go to school.

Some Saturday nights when Norman worked the night shift, Aunt Betty took me to ride on his bus just before his shift ended. On the way home we stopped by the open-air food stall in the market. We sat on stools by the stall and had noodles in soup with fish balls. At that time it cost 30¢ for a small bowl and 50¢ for a large bowl. Two or three times Norman took Aunt Betty and me to the bus drivers' club where I had Jell-O.

Aunt Betty and Norman talked about immigrating to America before Hong Kong would be handed back to China. They planned their exit well in advance. They might make a better living there. They said they would work at restaurants peeling potato skin if they had to until better jobs came along. They would take me along with them. They had also mentioned going to Borneo to take up nursing.

Mommy did not like us to make friends but allowed us to play with Peter and Daisy's five children. We liked to play house. One afternoon Amy, John, and I cooked something over an empty can filled with burning coal. Then we put rice, tomato, and water into a small toy clay pot on the makeshift stove to make congee. It turned out quite tasty. I was proud of the finished product through our joint effort.

One afternoon I got her permission to go to my classmate's house after school. I stayed there for too long. When I came home it was dinnertime. I did not have my own house key. Mommy sent Heather to the door to tell me that I was not allowed in. There was a locked folding metal chain door in front of the main door. That door opened in the middle. Fortunately I was tiny so Heather held open both sides at its bottom part and I crawled in. Mommy did not say anything but her face turned black.

Mommy never asked me to do any housework. She delegated it to Heather who was not shy and quiet like me. Heather thought it was not fair to have her do all the work. Mommy said to me to wait till I was married to do housework. She was not doing me a favour because I did not have the chance to practise housekeeping.

As time went by, I found out that I did not like the way Mommy handled things. She did not know how to manage money. So I said to myself that when I grew up, I would have a sound financial plan. I did not like how she talked to me either. I found that she rubbed people the wrong way. I tried hard not to copy any of the flaws in her character. She had an inferiority complex. She was sensitive and negative due to the fact that she was a concubine's daughter. She and I had a communication gap. As shy and quiet as I was, I would stand up for myself when Mommy said something I did not like or agree with. I would put up resistance and would not hesitate to voice my opinions. I frequently clashed with her. I was rebellious even as a young girl. I had a strong head too. Mommy found that I was a problem child. In a way, I learned everything from Mommy. I did things by turning completely around the way she handled them. I yearned for a happy family. When I had children of my own I would shower them with love and affection.

When Uncle Bob finished high school at around twenty years old, he began working in a Hong Kong government department. He saved up some money and bought a tabletop record player. The very first singer I heard on his record player was Patti Page. When he was not home I played songs from his record collection. Sometimes I listened to English hit songs playing on the radio. The popular singers at that time were Elvis Presley, Ricky Nelson, Neil Sedaka, Paul Anka, Gene Pitney, Peggy Lee, Connie Francis, etc.

When I was eleven years old, I was home from school earlier than David and George so Mommy sent me to take David and George home from their school, which was in the central district. I took a bus from Wanchai, got off on Garden Road, and walked up to the mid-level to the school, which was almost across from the governor's house on Caine Road.

Before I headed out to my brothers' school, I changed from my school uniform to a cheongsam-style top with matching pants. I wore a pair of wooden clogs with a two-inch-high heel. This was the cheapest type of casual footwear Mommy could afford to buy me. They were sold in stores in the market. We could choose different kinds of flaps to put over them. My hair was down to my waist at that time. I tied it up in a bun before I headed to my brothers' school.

I was in grade 6 in 1959 and had to write a general grade 6 examination before the end of the school year. I failed and had to repeat the grade.

Near the middle of 1959, Uncle Edward sold the cinema so Papa was out of a job. Uncle Edward held a high position at the Hong Kong Jockey Club where Papa worked part-time on the weekends when the horse races were on. I did not know how Mommy got by with less money every month but she must have realized he did not have a full-time job, so she did not act hysterical towards him.

On Chinese New Year day 1960, Aunt Betty gave me her old leather purse. I turned it upside down to empty the debris and dust. A mirror fell out from it and broke. Mommy gathered the broken pieces and put them in a red Chinese envelope, which was used to give out money as a gift to children during Chinese New Year.

One Saturday morning soon after the Chinese New Year, I was still sleeping with the blanket covering my face. Papa wanted some water stored in a flask in our room. When I heard him, I pulled the blanket away from my face and had a look at him before I went back to sleep.

That night I went with Aunt Betty and Norman to see a Chinese movie. It was about an orphan girl around my age. In the movie this girl sang a song that went something like "Only mothers are nice in this world. The children who have mothers do not know that. If they do, where else can they find happiness?" Aunt Betty and I kept crying all through the movie. When we got home we were told Papa was in the hospital. He fainted while walking home after work. Early the next morning, Mommy and Aunt Betty went to the hospital to be with Papa. He had a brain hemorrhage. The doctor could not do anything to save him. He never regained consciousness and died that morning. Aunt Betty told me later that right after Papa died, Mommy fell down in front of his death-bed. She cried out loud and asked what she was going to do with five young children in tow. Papa died at the age of forty-six after decades of alcohol consumption, which took its toll. Mommy was thirty-seven years old and I was thirteen years old. All of us sib-lings were born two years apart except for Jane who was five years younger than George and she would turn three years old in twenty days when Papa died. I thought that the mirror I broke earlier really brought bad luck.

Before Mommy and Aunt Betty got back home, a man from a funeral home came to see us and broke the bad news to us. He wanted our business. Ah mah started to cry after she learned of her son's death. She kept on crying all day long. She was seventy years old at that time. I did my best to comfort her even though my young world was shattered abruptly. I told her that I would work hard at school and get a good job when I grew up. She finally stopped crying that night so Heather and I could get some sleep. We left the light on all night as ah mah stayed up to watch us sleep. When we got up the next morning, ah mah told me that Heather and I lay very still as we slept.

On the day of the funeral, ah mah told my siblings and me to call out "Papa" in front of him because that would be the last time for us to do that. It was an old Chinese custom that white-haired people did not go to the funeral of black-haired people. Ah mah stayed home all by herself. Uncle Edward paid for the funeral expenses. Jane slept through the ceremony because it was her nap time. Papa was buried in a cemetery in the New Territories.

Another old Chinese custom is that when any of the parents die, for about one month, as a sign of mourning, the daughter will wear in her hair a small white flower woven with woollen yarn. The son will attach a small piece of black cloth in front of his shirt pocket. David and George went back to school the day after the funeral. I stayed home for an extra day so I took my two brothers to school. Jane went along with me. As we were walking up to the school, we met a housemaid who stared at us sympathetically. After I dropped my brothers off, Jane and I took the bus home. Jane sat on my lap and had her nap on the bus. Once again the fare conductor looked at us sadly. The white flower fell from Jane's hair and I was not aware of it until we got back home. As Jane grew older she said she had no recollection of Papa at all.

Right after Papa died, I felt a sense of loss and melancholy and there was a void in my life, although he was not around most of the time when he was alive. He worked seven days a week with no holidays. Uncle Bob told us not to think he had died but he had gone to America to make a better life for us.

One evening soon after Papa passed away, porh pawh, Uncle Bill, and Uncle Bob joined us for dinner. Halfway through, Uncle Bob announced that he would give Mommy $400 every month to support us. As soon as I heard this, I understood that being the oldest child it would be my turn to take over the role of supporting my family when I grew up. I would be the father to my brothers and sisters. I was a girl with a mission.

In order not to take Uncle Bob's money for free, Mommy cooked for porh pawh and her siblings and we all had dinner together every night. That meant more and better food, which was a welcomed change.

At dinner one night, Uncle Bob told me to have more rice since I was growing. Sometimes Daisy's servant gave me some bread crust she cut out to make sandwiches for Amy and John's school lunch. It satisfied my hunger.

Soon after Papa died, Mommy said to me while we were having dinner that because I was holding my chopsticks with my left hand when we were supposed to use our right hand, it was like a sword fight between me and the person sitting on my left side. She implied I was in Papa's way and that was why he died. I felt very hurt on hearing this. It was not my fault to be born left-handed. How could she say such a cruel thing to me? In order not for her to be leery that she might be the next to die because of me, I made myself hold the chopsticks with my right hand. If it were Heather who liked to talk back and was not timid like me, she would say to her "Why don't you blame yourself instead. It was you who jinxed him to death after years of badgering and nagging him and quarrelling with him."

One afternoon at school, I was summoned by an office clerk to meet a visitor. He was a young Chinese man who introduced himself as Mr. Wu from a reputable Chinese newspaper publication company. There were scholarships donated by the Hong Kong Jockey Club where Papa worked part-time before he died. These were for needy students to apply through this company. Mr. Wu dealt with the administration of these scholarships. He said to me that an anonymous person who knew us contacted them about our situation. He told me that for the rest of the school year the school fees for the four of us brothers and sisters would be taken care of. Aunt Betty later found out the anonymous person was an English woman who befriended Norman when she took his bus regularly. He told her about us. Aunt Betty and Norman took me to meet her. She gave me her daughter's brown leather Clarke shoes which she outgrew. I had to wear black shoes to school so I turned them black with liquid stains. By wearing these good brand-name second-hand leather shoes, I grew up with big, nicely shaped and wide feet, contrary to ah mah's small bound feet.

I passed the repeated grade 6 public school examination at the end of the school year and went on to grade 7. Before school started, I went to see Mr. Wu about the scholarships for the coming school year for my siblings and me. I was granted the scholarship again but not any of my siblings because they did not do well in their previous school year.

Mommy wanted to find a job to make some money for the first time in her life. Since she had only an elementary education, there were not too many jobs available to her. There was another English lady who was also a passenger on Norman's bus and was a volunteer for her church. She was responsible for feeding the poor children living in our neighbourhood with free milk. Through Norman, Mommy got the job of getting the milk ready every morning from Monday to Friday. When all the milk was distributed around noontime, Mommy washed all the cups and the floor. The pay was low but there was something for her to do. One of the English ladies who volunteered there, Mrs. Martin, offered her a job at her home in the central district. She did ironing for her family for three afternoons a week.

Mommy also got a job at a free dental clinic at our local community centre every Friday evening. She assisted the dentist and cleaned the dental equipment. One Friday I needed a filling in a cavity at the clinic. The receptionist failed to show up, so Mommy told me to take over to register patients and myself. All these years growing up in Hong Kong, I never paid to see a dentist, I relied on free clinics. I went to one run by a Protestant church nearby whenever I required dental care.

After work on weekdays, Mommy took David and George to school which was close to Mrs. Martin's house. After dropping off David and George and she was free that afternoon, she played mah-jong at one of the players' homes, which was right next to the school. All the players were mothers whose sons went to the same school. They stopped the game when school was over. When she was not playing mah-jong, she came back home and had her afternoon nap. On some evenings she played mah-jong with our neighbours until late at night.

Several months after Papa died, Aunt Betty broke up with Norman. Porh pawh was delighted. She thought it was good riddance. Aunt Betty realized that she would not have a bright future if they got married. She and Norman did not have good-paying jobs. She gave Mommy $100 every month after Papa died. Norman decided to leave Hong Kong and start a new life for himself in England where he took up nursing.

Right before the first Christmas following Papa's death, Mommy, Peter, Daisy, Amy, John, and I went up to the third level for a walk. About thirty minutes into our walk, we looked back and saw a middle-aged man in only an undershirt and long pants with a chopping knife in his hand. There was no one else around except our group of people. We all thought we were in big trouble. He might try to harm us. After a short while he stopped following us, but turned and walked up the slope where there were many evergreen trees. He chopped down a tree for the purpose of selling it as a Christmas tree. We all breathed a sigh of relief.

Through a fellow female teacher, Aunt Betty met a businessman whose name was Harold. He owned a tailor shop and a shoe store in Tsim-Sha-Tsui, the tourist district in Kowloon. When Peter Lawford, the Hollywood actor, visited Hong Kong, he shopped at his shoe store. His photo with his autograph was displayed in the front window of the store. Harold was divorced and had two teenage children, one daughter and one son. His ex-wife left their two children in her aunt's care. She then went to Germany with another man. Harold was thirteen years older than Aunt Betty. He wanted to remarry and started to date her. They went out after his stores closed late in the evening to have dinners at the restaurants. Aunt Betty often brought leftovers home for us to feast on before we went to bed. Sometimes they went to the movies. One night they took me along to see *European Nights* featuring performances in nightclubs all over Europe. The Platters were in the movie performing their song "Harbour Light."

Harold had a car. When he took time off on Sunday he drove Aunt Betty, my siblings, and me for rides all over Kowloon and the New Territories. Afterwards we had dinners at some pricey restaurants. I had a taste of what life was like with money.

After dating for two years, Harold and Aunt Betty got married. They bought a condominium apartment unit near Harold's stores. I found him a much nicer man than Norman. He kept on taking us on outings every Sunday afternoon.

When I was in junior high school, porh pawh stopped going to see Cantonese operas. Her most favourite actor, the "Love Monk," had retired. She took me to watch Chinese movies instead. We usually went for the noon shows on Sundays. Sometimes after the shows, we went to have a late dim sum lunch at a restaurant where there was a female and a male performing Cantonese opera songs to entertain us. On two or three occasions, I wanted to watch old Hollywood movies instead. We saw *A Summer Place* and *The Prisoner of Zenda*. During one of the movies I looked at porh pawh and found she had fallen asleep. She must have been bored not knowing what the movie was about.

I befriended a classmate in grade 7. Her name was Catherine and she was several months older than me. Her ancestor came from Shandong, the same province Confucius was from. We were of the same height and weight. Other classmates called us twins.

One weekend Catherine and I joined a retreat and sleepover at another Catholic girls' school. I asked Aunt Betty to let me bring along one of her store-bought pajamas, which was more presentable than my worn-out ones.

Catherine had an older brother who was attending medical school in Australia. She planned to join him after grade 8. She would attend secondary school in Australia for one year to brush up her English before she took up nursing. She asked me to go with her. Instead of talking over to Mommy, I turned to porh pawh who told me that she would discuss this with Uncle Bill and Uncle Bob. When I came home from school the next day, porh pawh said that both my uncles thought I might be afraid at the sight of blood, which was true. I hardly had to do housework so far in my life. The thought of having to take care of patients did not appeal to me. Anyway, it would cost a lot of money for the trip to Australia and the fee for the year in secondary school in Australia would be astronomical.

Mommy liked to pick on ah mah when she needed someone to quarrel with. Ah mah was fed up with this. She said to us grand-children that she wanted to move to a senior citizen's home. I was around fifteen years old at that time and did not know how to help her. She found that the tension between Mommy and her became more and more difficult for her to cope with. She felt trapped and there was no way out.

She was distraught and one morning she left home and did not come back until dinner time. She later told me she walked all the way that morning to the harbourfront where she stopped and reflected on the life she was living, but realized that there was nothing within her power to change things. She had to bow to her fate. She stood there for hours and caught the attention of a police-man who then approached her to find out if she needed help. Ah mah told him about the relationship between Mommy and her. He then persuaded her to go back home. Shortly after I had a talk with Heather, David, and George. I said to them that if ah mah was to go to a senior citizens' home, we would all go to an orphan-age. One night the four of us confronted Mommy on this subject. She was furious and mad at us. We had a heated argument with her. She considered me the ringleader. Porh pawh, Uncle Bill, and Uncle Bob were home and heard what was going on but they did not intervene. When Aunt Betty found out what happened from porh pawh, she offered to take ah mah into her home. There was a tiny servant's quarter where she could stay. This was a good solution for everyone concerned.

For the first time in a long time, there was some peace and quiet in our family. I tried my best to keep a low profile in order not to become Mommy's next target to vent her anger. I avoided being taunted by her at all costs. I was in her bad books already. I could not wait for the day when I was old enough to leave home and become independent.

In my senior high school years, I liked to hang around with three or four of my classmates. One of them was a competitive swimmer who swam across the Hong Kong harbour a few times. She had an athletic build. Every morning before class, we gathered around in the schoolyard. My classmates talked and laughed. I stood among them and listened, though I tried hard to say just the word "yes" but never got around to uttering it.

In my teens, porh pawh stayed home most of the time as she was getting older and had health issues. She went out only to have dim sum lunch. She was particularly fond of an item made up of three round layers with a slice of white steamed bun in the bottom, a piece of lean barbecued pork in the middle, and a slice of barbecued pork fat on the top. It was called Gold Coin Chicken without the chicken.

I was special to porh pawh. She gave me a monthly allowance of $20. With the money, I went to movies with Heather once in a while. Heather and the rest of my siblings got their allowances from Mommy.

In 1962, porh pawh's two houses in Ap Lei Chau burned down. She put the lot left vacant after the fire up for sale. Soon there was a conditional offer with a deposit of $40,000, but the deal fell through and the deposit was forfeited. Porh pawh became richer with a large amount of money, and she gave her three daughters $1,000 each. With the money, Mommy bought herself a diamond eternity ring for $700.

In the early 1960s, I listened to a lot of English pop songs. During the summer holidays, I did my school assignment with the radio on. They played songs mostly by the Beach Boys, Paul Anka, and Cliff Richard with his band the Shadows. I saw Cliff Richard's movie *Summer Holiday*.

One Sunday afternoon, when I was fifteen or sixteen years old, I suddenly had a thought that homosexuality was natural. We hardly talked about this subject at the time. I had no idea why this thought occurred to me and I ignored it.

Soon after Aunt Betty got married, Uncle Bill, who was working in an office at a school, started dating a lady teacher at the same school. Her name was Susan. They got married in 1963. Before their wedding, Mommy sewed dresses for us sisters to wear to the wedding. She made me a red dress. Chinese brides wear red which is a sign of good luck. I was not the bride, so I absolutely refused to wear that dress to the wedding. Mommy insisted, but to no avail. She finally gave in and bought me a grey and pink dress. Uncle Bill watched what was unfolding. He did not like my stubbornness. I saw him staring at me with a disgusted look.

On November 22, 1963, we were shocked when we heard that President John F. Kennedy was assassinated in Dallas, Texas. Heather and I watched the funeral onscreen at the American consulate in the central district.

I watched many Hollywood movies all through my teenage years, movies such as *The World of Suzie Wong* on location in Hong Kong starring William Holden and Nancy Kwan. I went to matinees that showed rerun movies. I watched *The Student Prince* and remembered vividly when the prince stood on the table singing Mario Lanza's "Drink, Drink, Drink." There were British actors and actresses in the Carry On movies. I liked the British comedian Terry-Thomas. I also saw many European actors and actresses in movies at that time. They were George Chakiris in *West Side Story*; Horst Buchholz in *Fanny* with Charles Boyer and Leslie Caron;

Capucine in *North to Alaska*; Marcello Mastroianni and Melina Mercouri in *Never on Sunday*; Christine Kaufmann and Gina Lollobrigida; Alain Delon in *Once a Thief* with Ann-Margaret. Another French actor Jean-Paul Belmondo was in a movie filmed on location in Hong Kong. I had never watched any of Brigitte Bardot's movies though.

One afternoon Heather and I went to see *The Longest Day* showing at a theatre near Fenwick Street, where there were many bars frequented by U.S. sailors on shore leave. The theatre was formerly the site of a funeral home. After the movie was on for a long time, I needed to go to the washroom. When I came out of the toilet, the washroom was packed with women. I was taken aback and blamed myself for loving to go to movies so much that I even went to a theatre which used to be a funeral home and was haunted by all these female ghosts roaming around the washroom. I rushed out to get back to my seat and as soon as I stepped back into the theatre I saw that the light was on. It was a long movie so there was an intermission, which was the first ever for me.

There were amateur song contests every summer in the 1960s. For many years, the contestants chose to sing Del Shannon's "Runaway" and some of them did quite a professional job.

In 1964, the music scene changed completely with the advance of the British invasion. I loved the Beatles. Every day I waited anxiously for their songs to be played on the radio. I liked most other British pop groups such as the Dave Clark Five, Gerry and the Pacemakers, the Searchers, and Manfred Mann. I liked to listen to Petula Clark, Nat King Cole, and Harry Belafonte also. Amy and John liked the Beatles too. They could afford to buy their records. When they played them, I stood in the hallway behind the closed door of their room and eavesdropped. When the movie *A Hard Day's Night* was in the theatre, John went with Heather, David, George, and me to see it. After the movie, we all had wonton noodles at a restaurant.

A year after Uncle Bill and Aunt Susan got married, Uncle Bob also tied the knot with a girl called Winnie. Uncle Bob had a part-time job teaching English in the evening at the school where Winnie was the student. She was nine years younger than Uncle Bob. After they got married they took over the room porh pawh, Heather, and I used to be in, and we moved into the room occupied by Mommy, David, George, and Jane. There were two bunk beds in the room. They were fitted with wooden planks as mattresses. Mommy and Jane slept on one of the beds in the bottom level. Heather and I were on the one above them. Porh pawh had the other bed in the bottom all to herself. David and George shared the one on the upper level.

Porh pawh hired a live-in servant just before Uncle Bob and Aunt Winnie got married to help with the extra work of the expanding family. The servant slept in the same room with us on a folding canvas bed. The eight of us crammed into a 12' by 15' room.

In the summer of 1964, porh pawh's house in the western district was damaged in a typhoon. The wall on the top floor collapsed due to the strong wind and heavy rain. The tenants had to be evicted and they demanded compensation. Uncle Bob hired a lawyer who was an Englishman called Ian Cameron to go to court for porh pawh. The morning of the proceedings, Uncle Bob asked me to go along with him to watch what was taking place. I did not like to go out so I declined. When they came home from the court later that day, Uncle Bob told me that the lawyer won the case for porh pawh. He researched and found that owners of houses which were built before a certain year did not have to compensate their tenants if these houses were destroyed by force of nature. Uncle Bob said that while Mr. Cameron was appearing before the judge, he put the weight of his body on one foot and later shifted the weight to his other foot. I could tell Uncle Bob was really impressed by that lawyer's performance.

By then porh pawh had already sold the empty lots in Ap Lei Chau. She had enough money to have the typhoon-ravaged apartment building demolished and rebuilt into a four-storey apartment building. She kept one floor for herself for rental income. She gave one floor each to Uncle Bill and Uncle Bob. Her oldest son, who moved back to China with his family during the Second World War, had died of lung cancer several years ago. On the suggestion of Aunt Betty, porh pawh gave his widow and her children the remaining floor. Uncle Bill collected the rent for them and sent the money to them every month. The economy in China was poor at that time. Porh pawh's small great-granddaughters in China were shoeless in the photo her daughter-in-law sent to us from China.

Heather and I wanted to make some pocket money during our summer holidays. The plastic industry in Hong Kong was in its heyday. We took home large garbage bags full of plastic parts to be assembled. It was not as easy as it sounded. It was hard on our fingers.

Aunt May's daughter, Rose, heard of places in the eastern part of the Hong Kong Island where we could take home unfinished woven gloves which needed to be stitched together and sweaters for us to sew beads and sequins on. This was a more desirable job. When we got paid, we had snacks at some family-run restaurants.

With more spending money at our disposal, one Sunday afternoon Heather and I went to lunch at a nice restaurant famous for its hot dogs, sandwiches, and ice cream. I knew what to have and asked Heather to order for me because I was shy and reluctant to talk to the waiter.

Some Sunday evenings, Heather and I walked to a large Japanese department store in Causeway Bay. We were not there to shop, but just browse around. On the way home, we dropped into a Chinese grocery store and treated ourselves with some pickled green onion tops.

From the lesson I learned from Mommy, who did not know how to budget, I was very careful with money and made sure I had some savings. I suggested to Heather that we should put our money in the bank to collect interest and she agreed. We opened a joint account at a local bank. Since we did not have much money for deposit, we were only young girls and not valued clients, the bank tellers did not provide us with courteous services and I found them intimidating.

When I went out in the heat and humidity during the summer holidays, I came home with headaches. The air conditioning inside the theatres and stores was set at a very low temperature, but once I stepped outside it felt like a sauna. I did not keep myself hydrated well and this caused my headaches. I lay in bed until dinnertime. I liked to lie down to read rather than sitting on the hardwood chairs. There was no sofa in our room.

For the first half of the 1960s, I watched a few of James Bond's movies. One weeknight, Mommy went with me to see *To Kill a Mockingbird*. This was a very rare occasion for the two of us. After the movie, we had some piping-hot food in a pot at a Chinese restaurant.

I remembered watching the epic *Lawrence of Arabia* and subsequently two other Peter O'Toole's movies: *What's New Pussycat?* and Joseph Conrad's *Lord Jim*.

Before the start of grade 11, Aunt Susan said to me, "Fong Ting, you will be in your last year of high school. Before you leave this good convent school, you should try to get Jane admitted in it."

Near the end of the summer holiday, I took Jane to see the vice-principal, Mother Sophia, from Italy. She made Jane write an entrance examination into grade 1. I did not hear from Mother Sophia at all, so on the first day of school, I talked to her and she said Jane failed the examination. I asked if she could do something for me. She then told me to bring Jane to see the principal, Mother Superior, after school that day. I went back to school with Jane and

Heather. I took Jane into the Mother Superior's office. She told me to leave so she could talk to Jane alone. After a while she asked me to go back inside and said that she would accept Jane into her school. The Mother Superior's secretary asked me if I wanted to buy a ready-made summer school uniform available in the office for Jane who had to start school the next day, so I bought it for $10 and she said to me, "Now that your sister is enrolled into our school, you better buy the uniform from the school too."

On the way home, I said to Heather and Jane, "If there is a will, there is a way." It was the first thing that I had made sure I would accomplish what I had set out to do.

One day at our grade 11 Biology class, we had to dissect a rabbit. One of our classmates suggested that we would barbecue the rabbit that night at her house. I turned it down because I refused to eat that poor animal.

At the start of grade 11, I knew it was time to work hard at school so as to pass the general public-school examination in Hong Kong in order to graduate from high school with certificates. I spent all my waking moments preparing for the mid-term examination right after the new year.

Amy and her boyfriend, Jason, were attending the Hong Kong University by then. Just before the Chinese New Year, there was a party held at their university one Saturday night. They planned to go and on the day of the party Amy asked me if I could also attend the party to be the substitute of a fellow student who got an upset stomach. I did not see any reason why I should not go, although I did not know how to dance. I did not have any nice dresses, so Amy let me wear one of hers. When we arrived at the party I met my partner, Alfred, who had an ordinary look with a slim build and not much taller than I. I managed with no trouble with the slow dances. I just let him lead me around the dance floor. In those days, the twist was the dancing craze. I did not need any lessons to do it. I was not really enjoying myself but I was not nervous, even though it was the first time I went to a party. After a while, he started a conversation. He told me his mother was dead and I told him so was my father. He said he had several younger brothers and sisters. His father was not working but he owned seven apartment units. He had a motorcycle and asked me if he could see me again on the third day of the Chinese New Year. I hated riding behind a motorcyclist. Besides, I had no time to date in my final year of high school. Mommy said again and again that on the third day of the Chinese New Year it was a Chinese custom not to see anyone who was not a family member, otherwise there was a chance that we would end up in a quarrel. So I turned him down by giving him that excuse.

When I got home after the party that night, Mommy was still awake. She asked me how it went. I said it was all right and my partner asked me for a date but I refused. Mommy said that I should accept his invitation.

The Italian nuns at our school stressed vehemently that they did not want their students to be seen going out with boys. I had every intention of obeying their wishes as long as I was attending their school. Anyway, the thought of being offered a date despite my ugly look gave me a comforting thought.

A girl named Tamara, who was a few years older than me and lived nearby, worked as a teller in a bank right after graduation from high school. She became crazy after being on the job for not too long. I watched her walking in our neighbourhood looking weird and talking to herself. My reasoning was that she had to deal with numbers and count money all day long, so that was enough to drive her insane. I came to the conclusion that I would never work in a bank.

After the Chinese New Year, I concentrated on my studies. The general public-high school examination took place in June. I passed the examination and obtained my high school graduation certificate. I did well in English, but ordinarily in all the other subjects. Anyway, I was relieved that at last I had graduated from high school and got closer to taking over Uncle Bob's responsibility to provide for my family.

During summer that year, Mr. Wu at the newspaper company contacted me. He said one of his friends was hiring people to sell encyclopedias. It would be strictly on commission basis. I told him that I would give it a try. I went to his friend's office in Happy Valley for an interview. I got the job. There was a team of ten salespeople made up of both males and females. I was assigned at first to two ladies around my age. They advertised on the newspapers for readers who were interested to fill out forms appearing on the newspapers with their names and addresses. We took these forms and went over to their homes to try to make sales. I had never thought of being in sales, but I wanted to see if I could sell something.

One afternoon, Mr. Wu phoned me at the office and asked, "Fong Ting, how are you doing on the job?" He sounded like Uncle Bob on the phone. He was so nice to think of me and tried to help me after all these years of processing my scholarship applications. I was just one of the applicants. He did not need to be concerned in helping me to find work after I graduated from high school. That made me feel like he was an uncle to me. I regretted later that I did not go to his office to thank him in person. After three months, I was the only salesperson who did not sell anything so I quit. I realized that I was not cut out for sales positions.

I then applied for a policewoman position. I got a letter from the police recruiting office instructing me to go to a designated location in the central district at a certain time on a certain day when a police vehicle would pick up the applicants and take them for a written examination at their office near Aberdeen. Uncle Bill encouraged me to go after the job. He said I was tall enough to be qualified as a policewoman, but porh pawh objected. She thought that it was a dangerous job. I knew it was not the right vocation for me because of my shyness and timidity, so I did not go for the examination.

I also applied for teachers' college and was accepted, but Mommy had another plan for me. She said that I should go to university. That meant I needed to go on to attend grades 12 and 13. I could not get any more scholarship after grade 11 from the newspaper company.

There was another way to obtain enough credits in order to be accepted at universities. To achieve that I could study at home and then write the General Certificate of Education Examination which took place once a year. I decided to get two credits for a start. It cost $40 for the registration. Neither Mommy nor I had the money. She told me to borrow from Uncle Bill. So I did that in front of Aunt Susan. I told him I would repay him even though in my mind I did not know when. I felt very embarrassed at that moment. I knew that it was not practical for me to further my education. It would take at least five more years before I could complete university. I did not want to impose on Uncle Bob any longer. He had his own family by then, and Aunt Winnie just gave birth to a baby boy. Also one of the sticking points was that I did not have the money to pay for the high cost of a university education. Mommy would most likely ask me to beg and borrow from porh pawh, Uncle Bill, and Uncle Bob, which I dreaded.

When she found out I did not want to further my study, she then insisted that I should go to the teachers' college. Aunt Betty and Uncle Bob both tried to enter that college but were not successful. Mommy did not want me to pass up the opportunity. I did not like to be a teacher who had to talk all day long and manage a whole class of students. When I told Mommy about that, she was very upset. For the whole week, she had a long face and she talked with a low voice, which was her way of showing she was displeased with whatever was bothering her.

I was eighteen years old at that time, still a teenager, and I pondered my future. It did not seem there were too many career choices available to me. The one job I could think of that did not require a lot of talking and dealing with people would be a stenographer/typist. I decided to take a one-year commercial course at a French convent school. The nuns there covered their hair with white wide brim head pieces resembling those worn by the nuns in the play "Les Miserables."

One Sunday afternoon, Amy, Jason, and I were standing on the balcony when Alfred, my partner at the university dance, appeared in front of us on the sidewalk. He was not on his motorcycle but walked up all the steps to our house. We all looked at him and he looked back but did not say anything, and when he saw me he turned right back and ran down the steps. He must have found out from Jason where I lived.

John was attending university when I was taking my commercial courses. He was in medicine that required him to own a skeleton for his study. He bought one which was the remains of an East Indian man and kept it in his room. I felt uneasy whenever I thought that there was a skeleton among us.

The commercial course consisted of shorthand, typing, and commercial correspondence. The school fees were $100 per month. For the first several months, I found a tutoring job through a relative. I was paid $100 a month which covered my school fees. The teacher suggested that we should practise typing at home. Uncle Simon was good at shopping for all sorts of merchandise, so I asked him to get me a second-hand typewriter. He found me an old manual Underwood typewriter. It was huge and heavy, but it served the purpose.

When the movie *Night of the Iguana* starring Elizabeth Taylor and Richard Burton was showing in the theatre, the school where Uncle Bill worked obtained a large quantity of tickets for the afternoon show for their students who were allowed time off to watch the movie. Uncle Bill bought a ticket, but could not go, so he let me take his place. He gave me some lunch money too. I skipped class that afternoon. Before the movie, I had wonton noodles for lunch at a noodle restaurant near the theatre. This restaurant was famous for its Chinese New Year coconut milk cake which was cut in thin slices, dipped in egg, and pan-fried. I had that for dessert.

While I was still taking my commercial courses, Princess Margaret and her husband, Lord Snowdon, visited Hong Kong. As usual when the British royal family came here, they went to the horse races at the jockey club on Saturdays. On their way, their limousine passed in front of our house. The very first British royalty I remembered passing by my house was Princess Alexandria and her husband. We lined up on the sidewalk for them to appear. I was wearing a white sleeveless cotton top with pink horizontal stripes and a black miniskirt. My hair was tied up in two ponytails, one on each side. As the motorcade approached, I saw Lord Snowdon sitting on the side where I stood. I was very excited and jumped up to wave at him. He turned his head to see what this teenage girl who gave him a rock star welcome looked like.

Around that time, Heather and some of her classmates joined a Catholic youth group consisting of both boys and girls of Heather's age. They met regularly at the youth centre. There were parties for occasions like Christmas and New Year. I went to the parties with Heather even though I did not like dancing, but by then I wanted to socialize more. Heather was good at dancing, especially the a-go-go which I could hardly do and I envied her.

One Sunday I went with Heather and the youth group onto a U.S. naval ship anchored at the Hong Kong harbour. There was a young American man in naval uniform on board. He looked like Gary Lewis, the vocalist of Gary Lewis and the Playboys. I told him so and he smiled.

Near the end of my commercial school year, Aunt Betty met a young Chinese couple who were her former renters. They told

Aunt Betty that they were immigrating to Canada. The Canadian government had loosened their immigration law to allow more immigrants into the country. When Mommy heard that she went over to the Canadian Immigration Department in the central district for the application form. She gave me the form to fill out. We applied to immigrate to Canada as a family. I did not know much about that country except that it covered a vast area of land north of the U.S.A. It was cold in the winter with a lot of snow.

Mommy and I took the completed form back to the Canadian Immigration Department after I got off class on a Saturday. It was right at noon when we reached it. A man stepped out of the office and was about to lock it up. I told him what we were there for. He then took our application form and put it inside the office. After a few weeks, we received a reply in the mail informing us that our application was rejected. Mommy, who was a widow, spoke hardly any English and did not have much education nor money, she was certainly not able to survive in a new country with five young children. Our hope of starting a new life in Canada was dashed.

Soon I completed my year at the commercial school and at the same time wrote my General Certificate of Education Examination and passed both subjects. I got two credits for grade 12. I then applied at the Hong Kong Government Employment Office for a stenographer/typist position. My application was successful and a few months before I turned twenty years old I started my first full-time job.

The government department I was working in was located in a brand-new office tower in the central district. I was the secretary of two middle-aged Englishmen. They held senior positions in the department. When the first Englishman I worked for walked into the office the first morning on my job, I was startled at how he looked strikingly like my late father. The suit he had on, the style of his hair, and his eyeglasses resembled the impression I kept of Papa. His name was Charles Harrison. He was soft-spoken and friendly. The other Englishman looked older than Mr. Harrison. His name was Richard Kelly. He was completely different from Mr. Harrison. He was quick-tempered and seemed restless. He hardly stayed in his office for long. Beside taking dictation and typing, I had to answer incoming phone calls for Mr. Harrison and Mr. Kelly when they were tied up. There were many clients who wanted to see Mr. Harrison. I had to screen them first before allowing them to meet him. There was a large amount of talking and public contact in this job much to my dislike, but I needed it to bring money home. My salary was HK$480 monthly. I took over from Uncle Bob to give Mommy $400 every month. Out of the remaining $80, I paid for transportation to and from work and sundry expenses.

Mr. Harrison was a very kind man. Every coffee break he asked me to order an Ovaltine drink for him from the canteen in our department and he told me to order and paid for a drink for myself also. I ordered a Coca-Cola which I did not have too often. After a while, I felt bad taking advantage of Mr. Harrison's generosity so I stopped having drinks at coffee break.

One afternoon Mr. Harrison took me out for a buffet lunch at a world-renowned hotel near our office. We had wine and caviar which were luxurious items I never had before.

When I was in grade 9, I made friends with two of my classmates, Bryna and Yvette. Once in a while we met for lunch or movies on the weekend. We went to see *Dr. Zhivago* together. Yvette taught at a primary school. Her aunt was living in Vancouver, Canada. She knew a Chinese couple who had a son in his twenties and was looking for a wife. His name was Henry. Yvette's aunt tried to be a matchmaker. She arranged for Henry to meet her in Hong Kong. They liked each other. He went back to Canada but returned to Hong Kong after several months to get married. Bryna and I were invited to their wedding. Soon after they got married, Henry headed back to Vancouver where he filed papers at the immigration department for Yvette to join him in Canada.

In the early part of 1967, there was a riot in Hong Kong due to labour unrest. One day while I was at work, I heard news that the rioters had showed up near our office building. It sent us workers into a frenzy. We were told not to go outside during lunchtime. Before the afternoon rush hours began, the rioters had dispersed but the traffic was in chaos. I got a ride home from Mr. Harrison. One of my friends who worked close by my office and lived in Wanchai had to take a rickshaw home.

After a few months working at the government department, I discovered that the Canadian Immigration Department had moved to the same building as my department. I figured that I had work experience so I could apply for immigration to Canada on my own.

When Mommy was working in Mrs. Martin's house, she mentioned to her about my plan to immigrate to Canada alone. Mrs. Martin then phoned the Canadian Immigration Office to find out if stenographers/typists would be qualified as immigrants. She was told that they were a penny a dozen in Canada. I sent in an application anyway and was accepted to go for an interview in several months. In the meantime, one of the Canadian immigration officers from Canada, Mr. Robinson, came to see Mr. Harrison periodically. One morning Mr. Robinson was sitting next to my desk to wait for his turn to see Mr. Harrison. I took the opportunity to tell him of my forthcoming interview at his department.

On the day of the interview, I told Mr. Harrison that I had a doctor's appointment that morning. I did not want him to know of my intention of the immigration yet. Aunt Betty and Uncle Harold had applied for immigration to Canada too, and their application was accepted but they wanted to wait longer before they would make their move. Aunt Betty went with me for the interview to talk about this with the Canadian immigration officer interviewing me. It turned out Mr. Robinson was the interviewer. I told him I did not have much money to bring to Canada, but Aunt Betty could help me financially if necessary. I was quite confident that my application would be approved and before too long I was proven right.

Aunt May and Uncle Simon decided to immigrate to Canada also. Their application was accepted too. They would go with their four children: Christopher, seventeen years old; Rose, fifteen; Penny, twelve; and Kenneth, six. They wanted to reside in Vancouver, British Columbia, where it was not too cold in winter. The destination of my choice was Toronto, since it was the largest city in Canada there should be more office jobs available, but Mommy wanted me to settle in Vancouver too so I would be with relatives and not be alone in a strange country. For once I listened to her. Our tentative departure date was early August that year.

I told Mr. Harrison the news. He felt sad but at the same time glad that I might be making a better life in Canada. I said to him, "When it is time for you to retire and go back to England, be sure to let me know where you will be settling down so I can go over to see you one day."

Before I left for Canada in 1967, there was a harrowing incident at the Kai Tak Airport in Kowloon. A Pan Am jet on takeoff overshot the runway and ditched into the harbour. Luckily all the passengers evacuated safely. A few days later, an American man came to see Mr. Harrison about some immigration matter. He told me that he was one of the passengers on that plane.

I resigned from my position at the government department one month before I immigrated to Canada. I said to Heather, "There are ten provinces in Canada. I will go to all ten provinces to find a stenographer job if I have to, and I don't believe that I can't find any in one of them."

I hardly had any money to buy the necessary things to bring to a new country. The most expensive and must-have item was a one-way plane ticket to Canada. Of course I did not have the money. The most likely person I could turn to was Uncle Harold. I told Aunt Betty about that. She said I had to ask him myself. The following Sunday afternoon, Uncle Harold drove Aunt Betty, all my siblings, and me for an outing. I waited for a chance for the request but found it very difficult. I did not enjoy the car ride at all. Finally Uncle Harold drove us back to his home. He got out of his car to let us all off. I stood beside the car and summoned all my courage to blurt out the words. Uncle Harold gave me a favourable reply. I was so relieved that I felt a heavy load had been lifted from my shoulders. I swore at that moment that no brothers or sisters of mine would have to go through what I just had to go through. When it was time for them to go to Canada I would pay for their airfares.

The next thing I had to get was suitcases. All I could afford were the cheap plastic ones. I bought a big rectangular red-checked clothlike one with a matching carry-on bag.

Mommy gave Uncle Bill and Aunt Susan a woollen blanket as their wedding gift. They never used it so they let me bring it to Canada. The parting presents from Uncle Bob and Aunt Winnie were a black leather coat and a raincoat. I brought my old clothes along and stuffed as many things as I could into the two bags. I exchanged the HK$1000 I had into the equivalence of CDN$200 to take to Canada.

During the few months before my departure from Hong Kong, the radio played the song "To Sir, with Love" and Scott McKenzie's "San Francisco" frequently. The last Warren Beatty film I watched in Hong Kong was *The Roman Spring of Mrs. Stone* starring the old Vivien Leigh as Mrs. Stone.

Uncle Simon and Aunt May decided to leave Hong Kong on August 10, amid the riot which was still going on. Uncle Simon got the least expensive plane tickets he could find for all of us. We flew on the Philippines Airline. I cried when I said goodbye to Mommy and my siblings.

Once the plane took off, we heard hit songs playing on the plane for our listening pleasure. This was the only means of in-flight entertainment back in those days. They must have deliberately played Tom Jones's "Green, Green Grass of Home" which made my eyes well up and I felt homesick already.

It was the first time I flew and the plane took the long route. There were several stopovers before we arrived at our final destination. The first stop was Manila, the Philippines. From there we flew to Guam. It was nighttime when we arrived there. We got off the plane and walked around the airport. I saw some American soldiers nearby and for the first time a vending machine selling Coca-Cola.

Soon after we left Guam, we crossed the International Date Line and headed for Honolulu over the equator. It was daytime when we were near Honolulu. When our plane was about to touch down, I looked through the window and saw that it was raining and down below there were a lot of lush green trees and beautiful tropical flowers. It was a pretty sight and I wished that one day I could go back there for a vacation.

We stayed in the Honolulu airport for a short duration and our plane took off for San Francisco. When we arrived there, I did not wear some flowers in my hair as in the song. Before getting onto our connecting flight, Rose, Penny, and I walked outside the airport terminal. Back home there were signs everywhere warning us to keep off the grass, so we trod carefully on the road right by the lawn, until a policeman in a patrol car drove up to us and yelled, "Walk on the grass."

Our next stop was Seattle. It was nighttime when we touched down there. As I was getting off the plane, there was a couple in their late twenties or early thirties with a small boy walking in front of me. The man was of African descent and the woman was Chinese. The man was holding the child's hand.

After a stopover in Seattle, we finally headed for our final destination, Vancouver, Canada. It was morning when we went through immigration procedures at the Vancouver airport, which I found not too big, and of a plain and simple structure.

When I left the airport and set foot on the soil of my newfound home to start another chapter of my life, I would not be twenty-one years old yet until a couple of months later. It was the centennial year in Canada and the year the world exposition was held in Montreal, Quebec. It was also the year of the summer of love.

One of Rose's classmates, Valerie, and her family had settled in Vancouver one year before. Rose asked her to arrange accommodation for us on our arrival. Valerie's father met us at the airport and took us to an east end motel he had booked for us. We occupied two rooms. One morning I heard for the first time the Bee Gees' song "Massachusetts" playing on the radio in one of the rooms on our floor. The volume was turned up so high that it was blaring all over the hallway.

We did not do much for the first couple of days we were in Vancouver because it was the weekend. Uncle Simon took us downtown. I could hardly see any skyscrapers around and I found that the city was not too populated. We had lunch at a cafeteria where I ate spaghetti for the first time ever. We went to Chinatown too. There were grocery stores, restaurants, and a Chinese bakery store called B.C. Royal.

During our stay in the motel, Uncle Simon and Aunt May searched frantically for places to rent or else the money they brought from Hong Kong would deplete when the bill for the motel stay became too big. After about ten days they found a room on the main floor and the basement below it from a young Chinese couple with a small son. Uncle Simon, Aunt May, and Kenneth shared the room. The rest of us stayed in the basement.

My cousins and I slept on a makeshift wooden bed. I was the only one who brought my pillow with me. Uncle Simon and Aunt May packed their household items and bedding stuff in containers to be shipped to them. It took time for them to get to Canada. After a few nights, Penny complained that sleeping without a pillow on a hard surface gave her headaches. So I let her use mine and I folded up some clothes as my pillow.

Soon after we moved into our new home, Rose and I went to check out the neighbourhood. I was wearing my high-heeled shoes, which hurt my feet after walking for not too far, so I took them off and walked barefoot. We went into a convenience store along the way and found that a can of Campbell's tomato cream soup cost 9¢ and a loaf of white bread cost 10¢.

We saw help-wanted posters outside the store. They needed workers to pick blueberries and strawberries. That Sunday, Rose, Penny, and I waited in a designated area for a truck to pick us up. It was early in the morning when it dropped us off at a blueberry farm. The three of us were handed a big tin bucket and would be paid $6 to fill it up. We picked from a big tall tree laden with berries. Since the blueberries were very tiny, it took us all day to make the bucket full. We split the $6 among us. It was the first $2 I made in Canada.

When I left Hong Kong, Yvette was still waiting for her visa for Canada to be approved. She gave me Henry's phone number. One day I called him and he came over that night to drive me and my cousins to the Pacific National Exhibition, which was taking place.

I was anxious to find a job. The first place I went to was the government employment agency. They sent me to a fairly big Chinese restaurant downtown for a hostess position. A Chinese woman interviewed me briefly while standing near the entrance. She turned me down flatly right there and then.

I looked for help-wanted sections in the newspapers next. There was an opening for a part-time dishwasher at a restaurant near downtown. The restaurant owner was German and he offered me the job. I relieved the full-time dishwasher who had the weekend off. I replaced her on Saturdays and Sundays. I would have time to look for other jobs on weekdays.

They wanted me to start working on Saturday that very week. I reported for work at 11:00 a.m. before the lunch-hour rush. The owner's wife, Giselle, told me to put on a white apron. My first duty was to sweep the sidewalk in front of the restaurant. Then I went across the street to a grocery store owned by a Chinese man to buy some produce. My next duty was to sweep the restaurant floor. Then I cleaned the toilet bowls in both the men's and women's washrooms just before the restaurant opened for business. For the duration of the lunch hours, plates, cups, and cutleries kept on piling up. I worked non-stop loading and unloading them. The loading part was not a problem. It was the unloading of the just-washed hot items that scalded my fingers and in no time they were chapped. When Giselle saw that, she gave me a Band-Aid to put over them.

When the lunch hours were over, I went outside the back of the restaurant, sat on a chair, and started to peel the skin of a big bucketful of just-boiled potatoes which were too hot to handle literally. Aunt Betty and Norman talked about peeling potato skin if they had to in their adopted countries. I was the one who actually had to do it soon after I landed in Canada.

I was not provided with a hot meal during the day but I was allowed to help myself with drinks and the dark chocolate cake. I had Sprite, which Giselle liked to drink frequently.

In the middle of the afternoon and before the dinner rush began, I was given a break. I went for a walk near the restaurant. After walking for a while, I came in front of an old stone building and people were sitting on the steps and I sat down too. I began to cry and ask myself how I got into such a mess. Back home I hardly had to lift a finger. I never thought I had to make a living as a manual worker. It was a rude awakening. I missed my brothers and sisters very much, but I knew very well that there was no turning back. The most urgent matter I faced at that time was to come up with at least the equivalent of HK$400 to send to Mommy at the end of that month. I would do anything to make the money. I then dried my tears, got up, and headed back to the restaurant.

There were three waitresses. They were of European descent. Danielle, a French lady, was very nice to me. I washed dishes non-stop until closing time at 11:00 p.m. Danielle's fiancé, a Chinese man from Macau, came to pick her up. After I had done all the dishwashing, Giselle cooked me a schnitzel, the specialty of the restaurant. This was something new to me and it was delicious particularly because it was very late at night and it was my only hot meal all day long. By the time I left the restaurant it was close to midnight. I went to take the bus home. I had to wait for at least thirty minutes because it did not run very often that late at night. The bus ride home took about thirty minutes. The next day I did the same thing all over again.

At the beginning of the following week, I felt sick, probably from working too hard and too long over the weekend. I stayed in bed for several days and ate hardly anything. Since I had not been in Canada long enough, I was not qualified for free medical care yet so I did not go see a doctor. I had a lot of sleep, hoping I would feel well enough on the weekend to go back to work. When I woke up that Saturday morning I still felt weak, but managed to drag my way to the restaurant. I told Giselle I had been sick and my appetite was not good. That night Giselle made me a cold-cut sandwich.

I spent the next week looking for office work at the government employment centre again. The officer who interviewed me found an opening for a manual job at a local hospital. I went there and filled out an application. I looked for jobs at the provincial government employment office too, but did not see any typing or clerical positions available. I also looked for work at one of the largest Canadian chartered banks downtown, but was turned away.

In September, all my cousins were enrolled in public schools. Christopher and Rose made friends with their classmates who were our neighbours. They liked to sing the song "Last Kiss" which was popular at that time, but they changed a few words to make it sound obscene. After school one afternoon, I went with Rose to her classmate's house. There was a pear tree in her backyard and she let us pick some ripe pears to bring home. One day I was walking home on a laneway and passed by a prune tree in someone's backyard with prunes hanging over the fence and some ripe ones fell on the ground. I gathered several of them and ate right there without washing them.

Meanwhile the riot in Hong Kong escalated. The rioters planted improvised explosive devices throughout the city. One of the well-known broadcasters at a local Chinese radio station got killed that way.

Aunt May was looking for jobs too and she found out some local farmers needed farm hands to pick cucumbers. Since I was not working during weekdays, I went with her to the farm. We waited at a certain location near our house and a truck came to drive us to the farm. We crouched all day long to harvest the crops lying in the field. We worked under the warm September sun. We did not wear any hats or put sunscreen on, not knowing that we might get sunburned this way. In the late afternoon, the truck dropped us off where we got on in the morning.

We went back to the farm the next day. Near noontime, the farm owner came and told me to pick potatoes instead. He asked me to come with one other person, so my aunt came with me. On the way home, a middle-aged Canadian man who sat next to me on the truck said that he would introduce a cowboy to me and I thanked him for that.

I got off work at the restaurant late Saturday night that week, and waited at the bus stop without a soul around. After a while an old-modelled car pulled up to me. The white male driver told me to get into his car. I hesitated, but he yelled at me and I did as he said without thinking. As soon as I was in the car he started talking and I could smell alcohol on his breath and sensed immediately that I was in big trouble. He asked me if I knew Alice Chan. I said no. He then asked, "Do you know what f - - k means?" I had heard that word before and knew its meaning, but I played dumb and said no. After driving for a short while, he stopped the car and told me to get out, probably because he knew Alice Chan so he would not harm any Chinese woman.

It was a close call and a frightful experience. After I jumped out of the car I was relieved, but I found myself in the middle of nowhere. I could tell it was a residential area. I saw there was a light on at one of the houses at the street corner. I walked near it and found out it was an auto body shop, which was still open. I went inside and there was a lone Canadian man working on something. I asked him if I could use his phone. He asked me if I was working at the nearby hospital and I said no. I told him I got lost. He helped me to find the phone number of a taxi company and a driver came soon after to take me home. As time went by, I was puzzled as to why the body shop was not located in a commercial area on a busy main street and why it was still open so late on a Saturday night. Anyway, I learned the lesson not to get into a stranger's car the hard way.

Yvette finally obtained her visa and reunited with Henry. They stayed in a house with Henry's old parents. Yvette soon found that her in-laws were not easy to live with but there was nothing she could do at the time. She also needed to send money every month to help with supporting her family back home. She had a cousin who was working at an optical store in Vancouver, and sometimes that store would hire people to work on the eyeglass frames. Yvette and I filled in application forms.

By that time Uncle Simon had found an electrical technician job at the airport so he wanted to move to a bigger place for all of us to stay. One weekend, Rose came across a vacant half of a semi-detached house. Uncle Simon liked the house and he signed the lease for one year. It was a two-storey house with three bedrooms. There was no bedroom available for me, so I slept on a foam mattress on the kitchen floor. Uncle Simon got hold of an old television and put it in the kitchen. I heard Jim Morrison of the Doors singing "Light My Fire" on television. At around that time the riot in Hong Kong was finally over.

After we had settled down in our new home I went to the Canadian Employment Office again. On leaving the elevator at the floor of the employment office, a young, good-looking Canadian man in his twenties with a baby face walked beside me and said, "You are pretty. I was on the bus and saw you walking on the sidewalk." I replied with a thank you and a smile. He then walked away. I did not understand why he said that to an ugly duckling like me. I might not be that ugly after all or else I would not attract the young man and made him get off the bus and follow me to have an up-close-and-personal look and to compliment me.

At the employment office there was an opening for a chambermaid at a hotel by the English Bay. I went there for an interview and was offered the position. I had to work both on weekdays and weekends. Rose wanted to work part-time and Giselle agreed to let her replace me.

On the first day on the job at the hotel, my supervisor said to me that many of the chambermaids who worked there were called either Mary or Maria and she asked me if I wanted to be called some other name instead. I answered that I wanted to change my name to Eleanor. When I told Christopher about this after work, he said that I named myself after the subject of the Beatles' song

"Eleanor Rigby," but that was the only name I could think of at that moment.

Before I started working, I put on my chambermaid uniform. Another chambermaid, a middle-aged Canadian woman, trained me. I was assigned ten rooms every day. It was hard work, needless to say, especially for me. I had to make beds, dust dressers, desks and night tables, vacuum floors, and wash bathrooms. It was a mad dash. I was overwhelmed.

A few days later my supervisor came into the room I was working on to evaluate me. She watched me as I was dusting the dresser which stood right against the wall. She then ran a finger between the dresser and the wall and showed me the dust on it. I was embarrassed.

I did not have to work one Friday and the Beatles' movie *Help* was showing in the theatre. I asked Rose to watch it with me but she turned me down. I did not want to go alone and I never got the chance to see the movie ever.

As the weather turned cooler in Vancouver, the hotel business slowed down. I was seldom called in to work. Uncle Simon suggested that I went to Seattle, Washington, which took only a couple of hours by Greyhound bus. There might be more office jobs available there. His neighbour in Hong Kong, Mr. Lam, moved there a few years ago. He had three daughters around Rose's age and the four of them were friends. Rose kept in touch with the three sisters after they moved to America. I went there a few days before the American Thanksgiving and stayed with them.

The three sisters would go to a town called Chehalis near Seattle for Thanksgiving. This was arranged by their school, which was attended mostly by immigrant children. Each student would be assigned to an American family for several days over the Thanksgiving holiday. Since there were rooms for more students, I went along with them. We were driven by buses to our destination. I was dropped off at a house where I was greeted by a middle-aged couple. They introduced themselves as Mr. and Mrs. Van Dyck. They had three children. The oldest girl was around thirteen years old. The younger girl was around eleven. The youngest one in the family was a boy around nine years old. Mrs. Van Dyck showed me my bedroom which was up in the attic. It was a nice big room with a comfortable bed and an electric blanket, which kept me warm and cosy all night. On Thanksgiving Day, I spent some time with the family and played board games with the children. Mr. Van Dyck was a lawyer. They invited their friends, an older couple, for Thanksgiving dinner. I sat across from the old couple at the dining table. The old lady asked me a few questions about myself and then remarked that I had good manners. I thanked her.

I celebrated my first ever North American Thanksgiving in Chehalis of all places, in such a big country and to have turkey at last was something I was thankful for.

There was a Goodyear Tire plant in town. Before we left Seattle two days after Thanksgiving, all the students went to have a tour of the plant. We were each given a Goodyear Tire mug and a replica Goodyear Tire keychain as souvenirs.

I left Seattle after a short stay. Instead of waiting for the hotel to call me back to work, I turned to the help-wanted column in the newspaper to look for another job. One morning I read on the front page of the newspaper that a woman got struck and killed in front of that hotel I worked at. I was shocked to see the victim was the Canadian woman who trained me on the chambermaid job.

It was near my first Christmas in Canada and I did not have a full-time job yet, but I managed to buy some cheap Christmas presents to send home. I also put one dry maple leaf inside the parcel.

We were in no mood to celebrate Christmas and New Year. Soon after the New Year Uncle Simon suggested again that I should go to Seattle to attend the community college there and work part-time after school. According to what he observed when he visited Seattle earlier, the economy in the U.S.A. seemed to be better than in Canada. There might be more jobs available there and I would be earning American dollars which were worth more when they were exchanged to Hong Kong dollars. I was persuaded by him and decided to try my luck in the United States. I took the Greyhound bus again and went to stay with the Lam's family temporarily.

I enrolled at the community college and took the English language course. The first Saturday I was there the three sisters took me shopping by the waterfront and we went near the Space Needle, which was the site of the World Exposition in Seattle. One evening after dinner, the oldest of the Lam daughters went with me for a ride in her friend's car. We got out of the car at a hilltop and stared at the night scene in the city. Snow started falling and I saw snow for the first time in America and not in Canada.

I did not know how to get around Seattle very well so I waited until I found my bearings before I started looking for work. While there I had my first peek of a computer on television. It looked like a tall filing cabinet. I also watched the Monkees, the Cowsills, and the Fifth Dimension on television. I heard that the smog was bad in Los Angeles.

I was at school for almost a month. I did not bring too many clothes with me. After school on the last Friday afternoon in January, I went back to Vancouver for the weekend. When I was alone with Rose, she told me that while I was in Seattle she phoned the youngest Lam's sister who told her that her mother was displeased with me. I lived with them without paying anything. I did not even help with doing the dishes. On hearing this I realized that I had overstayed my welcome, but without a job I could not afford to move out of their house yet. I bought some dried Chinese food stuff in Vancouver to give to Mrs. Lam in hope of easing some of her ill feelings towards my freeloading on her family.

That Sunday morning I got on the Greyhound bus to head back to Seattle. I brought my carry-on bag which I stuffed with as many of my belongings as possible. I even took my woollen blanket along. When the bus stopped at the border crossing, an American immigration officer got on board and when he stood in front of me and saw my bulging bag, he suspected that I intended to stay for a long time in America. He said to me, "You can stay in the States for two weeks."

Before class began the next morning, I went to see the vice-principal who was a middle-aged African American woman and told her what the immigration officer said. She replied immediately, "Don't worry. All the teachers told me that your English is very good and does well in class. Leave the matter to me."

On Wednesday that week, Uncle Simon called and told me that the spectacle store in Vancouver asked me to go for an interview the following Monday. I thought over it for a long time. My goal to come over to North America was not to go back to school. If I stayed in Seattle, I would be working part-time after school. I would not be making too much to support myself and my family back home. Besides, it would take me longer to sponsor my siblings to immigrate to the States before I could establish my residency status. I decided I would go back to Vancouver for the job interview.

I went back to Vancouver two days later. When I arrived at the Greyhound bus station in Vancouver I called Yvette on the pay phone.

I said, "The spectacle store asked me to go for an interview on Monday. Did they tell you to go too?"

Yvette replied, "No, they didn't."

I asked, "Do you want to go with me?"

Yvette said, "Let me check with Henry."

She came back to the phone after a minute and said, "Henry said that I shouldn't go with you. It may diminish your chance of being hired."

When I got back to Uncle Simon's house, I told him of my decision.

The next morning I thought further ahead into the future. It was very hard to find decent jobs in Vancouver. I had looked for six months and I might land a full-time job, which was not in my field. When my brothers and sisters were here, they would face the same problem. I decided to take a giant step to move on to Toronto, which was a bigger city with more opportunities certainly.

Before dinner that night, I broke the news to Aunt May. She gave me the phone number of Victor, who was Uncle Simon's former co-worker in Hong Kong. He immigrated to Canada and settled in Toronto a few months earlier. He was also Yvette's neighbour in Hong Kong and was invited to her wedding reception where I met him.

Aunt Betty's former classmate, Ethel, was residing in Toronto at that time too. I made a long-distance call to her and told her that I was on my way to Toronto soon.

I managed to hold onto the CDN$200 I brought with me up until then. I sent half of it to Mommy for my contribution for that month. With only CDN$100 left over, it was not enough for a one-way plane ticket to Toronto. All I could afford was to travel by train. I would leave Vancouver the following Monday night and arrive in Toronto on Friday the same week. I phoned Ethel again and informed her of my scheduled arrival. She said she would pick me up at Union Station. I then phoned Victor and gave him Ethel's phone number so he could contact me. Lastly I called Yvette. I said to her, "I will leave for Toronto on Monday. I won't be going for the interview at the spectacle store. Why don't you go and take my place?"

Yvette replied, "I will go, then. If you need money to take along with you, I can give you some."

I replied, "I'll be all right. Thank you anyway."

After I paid for my train ticket, I was left with CDN$30 and change to take to Toronto. I figured that if I ran out of money, I would go to the Catholic church for assistance. Being new in Canada I did not know I could seek help at the Canadian government social welfare office.

Uncle Simon drove me to the train station Monday night. Aunt May, Rose, and Penny came along too. Rose and Penny were sad to see me leave. After living together with them for six months we became very close. Rose cooked me a few chicken drumsticks and gave me several Tetra Paks of apple juice to take along. I made some luncheon meat sandwiches also.

I climbed onto the train and hence commenced my trek to uncharted territories in the east, assuming the part of a pioneer woman. I travelled economy class, needless to say. I had to sleep sitting up. The next morning I looked outside the window from the train, it was all covered with snow. I was in no mood to watch the magnificent Rocky Mountain Ranges as the train chugged by them. I sat on my seat almost all day. I did not bring any reading materials. I ate all the chicken drumsticks at the end of the second day. When I was hungry the next day, I reached for the remaining luncheon meat sandwiches and found that they were covered with mould. I was not aware that meat products had to be refrigerated. I would not buy any food on the train with the little money I had. I just drank the apple juice.

That night, the two older men of Eastern European descent who sat facing me got off the train. On their way out one of them handed me the pillow he rented on the train. I was touched by his kindness. I felt comfortable to have a pillow to rest my head on while sleeping, even though it was the last night of my train ride.

The train pulled into Union Station in Toronto at 7:30 a.m. Friday, February 15, 1968, a day after Valentine's Day. Ethel and her husband were waiting for me at the arrival area. They took me back to their apartment. Ethel made breakfast for me. She said that employers would not bother hiring people on Friday. I might as well get some rest. I lay down for the first time in several days on a pullout sofa bed in the living room and slept until dinnertime. Before I had dinner I phoned Victor. He said he would come over that night. He lived in a rented room in a house in Chinatown and he would give up that room and let me stay there. He would move in with two of his friends who were renting a flat in a house right across the street.

After dinner, Victor came with three of his Chinese friends. The night before I arrived, Victor told these friends that he would go to pick me up at my friend's place. Just before Victor was on his way, he called to let me know that he would show up soon. When one of his friends saw Ethel's name in Victor's address book he said he knew her for many years through her younger sister who went to the same university as he did in Ottawa. His name was Madison Liu.

One of Victor's friends drove us to Chinatown. I went up with Victor to what used to be his room on the second floor. I did not tell Victor that I could not afford to reimburse him for the rent. I needed to hold on to whatever money I was left with for as long as I could.

The next day Victor showed me around the city. When we were downtown, I saw many skyscrapers and office towers. The streets were filled with pedestrians and shoppers carrying bags of merchandise. I found Toronto very vibrant compared to Vancouver.

Victor studied at a technical college in Hong Kong. He was an electrical technician like Uncle Simon. Many of his classmates immigrated to Canada at around the same time as he did and settled down in Toronto. They lived close together in Chinatown.

After coming back from downtown, Victor took me to see his friend Edward. He lived with his mother and an older sister. When they found out that my last name was the same as theirs, which was not quite a common Chinese surname, they immediately made me feel I was part of their family.

I spent Sunday with Victor at the home of one of his other friends who cooked dinner for us. There I met a Chinese female immigrant, Gloria, who hung around with Victor's group of friends. She worked as a counter girl at a dry-cleaning store. Madison was present also.

After dinner, Gloria invited me over for lunch the next day. She also lived in a rented room nearby. She said she would take me to the government manpower office downtown after lunch. During lunch, Gloria told me that Madison told one of their friends in common that she looked sweet when she smiled and that one other friend showed interest in her too. Whenever they gathered for dinners, they arranged for Gloria to be seated in between her two admirers.

Since Chinatown was close to downtown, we walked to the manpower office. An officer there interviewed me and gave me a typing test right away. After the test, she said there was an opening for a typist at a bank, the same bank in Vancouver I went to apply for but was turned away. The next morning I went by myself for the interview. The personnel officer gave me a typing test. After the test she told me to report to one of her bank branches for work the next morning. I was elated, although I did not want to work in a bank in case I might become crazy like Tamara back home, but after months of searching for an office job in Vancouver, I finally landed one with no difficulty in Toronto. I could not be too choosy. I found an appropriate position on my first try. I wrote home about the good news immediately. At the end of that month I sent home CDN$110. I stipulated specifically to Mommy in the letter that I sent an extra CDN$10 to repay Uncle Harold for the plane ticket. I would keep on doing that until I paid him back in full.

Banking was a new experience for me. I certainly liked the opportunity to learn something different. The pay was low but there were free banking service fees, all kinds of staff benefits, and a full-course meal for lunch at the bank cafeteria cost less than $1.

After a short time on the job, my supervisor praised my typing as fast and accurate and said she was very pleased with my performance.

I went out for a walk during lunch hour one afternoon. I passed by a newsstand and saw the headline in a newspaper that Pierre Elliott Trudeau, who was running for the federal Liberal leadership, then would speak at the Toronto new city hall at noontime within days. When that day came I headed over there, which was close to my bank. Before I could get close to blocks away from where the speech took place, policemen directed people to turn back because the crowd was too large. It must have been the effect of Trudeaumania. Mr. Trudeau won the Liberal leadership and eventually the following federal election to become the prime minister. I started to pay attention to Canadian politics.

Nancy Greene won the female downhill ski gold medal for Canada at the Winter Olympics that year. To celebrate her victory there was a ticker-tape parade downtown. As it passed right by our bank, we stopped working to watch.

Rose sent me a letter from Vancouver soon after I moved to Toronto. Enclosed was a coveted American green card obtained for me by the vice-principal of the community college in Seattle.

One weekend in the beginning of March, we all gathered in Edward's apartment for dinner. Before we went home, Madison approached me and said he would attend a friend's wedding in Ottawa the next weekend. Ethel's two younger sisters and their mother were living in Ottawa at that time. I met them in Hong

Kong. He asked if I would like to go to the wedding with him so I could see Ethel's family. I accepted his invitation.

I left with Madison in his second-hand car the night before his friend's wedding. We stayed with Madison's good friend in Ottawa. They went to the same high school in Hong Kong and when they mentioned the name of the school, Jason went to that school also. I asked Madison if he knew him. Madison replied that they were classmates.

We attended the wedding ceremony in a Catholic church in the afternoon. Before the wedding reception that evening, Madison drove me to see Ethel's sisters and mother. We went back to Toronto that Sunday.

One week later, Madison asked me out to a movie and we started dating. I figured he was a friend of Ethel and her family and Jason's classmate, I could not go too wrong to be his date.

He was four years older than me. He had a medium build, an ordinary look, and did not have a baby face. He was five-feet-nine-inches tall, six inches taller than me.

When I found out about pizza, he took me to an Italian restaurant in Chinatown to try it and I loved it.

One morning at work there was some document I had to deliver to another department, which was one floor below the banking floor I was on. It had to be in joint custody. I went with another co-worker. We stopped in front of the counter of that department. A young man and an older man came over to us. My co-worker introduced us. The young man's name was Andrew Smith. He said hello to me with an English accent. He had an innocent baby face resembling a mini version of Warren Beatty. He was wearing dark-rimmed glasses. He was in his twenties, of medium build and height. The older man's name was Wolfgang Koch.

Madison graduated from a university in Ottawa in 1967. He had a bachelor's degree in engineering. Later that year he found an engineering job at a big food company manufacturing snacks and beverages. He shared a flat in Chinatown with two university students who were brothers from Hong Kong.

We went to the movies on the weekends. We still had dinners every night with Victor and his friends at their flat. One night I watched Sidney Poitier's *Guess Who's Coming to Dinner* on television after dinner. Spencer Tracy, Katharine Hepburn, and Katharine Houghton were in that movie too.

Since Andrew Smith and I did not work on the same floor and there were no more documents to be delivered to him, I did not see him again for a while until one day when I went downstairs and passed by his department. I looked inside and saw him working away at his desk with his head down.

Soon it was springtime when young men's fancy turned to love. At work one morning, Andrew Smith appeared in front of my desk out of the blue.

He asked me, "Do you want to go with me to work in Hong Kong?"

He had made an audacious move. He must have been desperate. He put me on the spot and I felt that time was constrained for me to respond to such a proposal. I did not realize that this was not to be taken slightly and any decision should not be made hastily. All I thought of at that time was I would not abandon all my siblings who were depending on me to get them out of Hong Kong. I was not footloose and fancy-free. The bridge had been crossed and there was no turning back. Too much was at stake.

I replied, "There was a riot in Hong Kong recently. It was not nice to go and work there."

That was the only answer that came to my mind readily. He turned and walked away immediately. Our paths never crossed again until one sunny summer Sunday afternoon when Madison and I went to a park. We were standing on the grass and when I looked to my right side, I saw Andrew Smith and a lady with white hair tied up in a bun walking down the pathway not far from where we were standing. He looked straight ahead, pretending he did not see me. He must have thought that the real reason I turned him down was that I already had a boyfriend. I stood still as they passed by. That was how Andrew Smith walked out of my life and walked into oblivion. It was a tragedy of Romeo and Juliet proportions, an English Romeo and a Chinese Juliet. From then on, a walk in the park was no cakewalk for me.

I should have been curious enough to approach him the next morning to ask about the lady he was with in the park. If I opened a dialogue, I would find out more about him. After all, we only knew each other's name. It might blossom into something magical and we would see eyeball to eyeball. Then poor Madison would get a Dear John letter from me.

For once I wished I had listened to my heart and not my head. I never saw Andrew Smith in the bank anymore. My encounter with him was brief. What could have been a miracle melted into a mirage. It was too good to be true. He is a mystery man in my life. He is history that forms part of the story of my life. It was never in my wildest dream that an ugly duckling I had considered myself to be since I was young, could have such a handsome secret admirer. His proposal popped up to haunt me from time to time.

In retrospect, any young woman who slammed the door shut on the face of Warren Beatty look-alike when he came knocking was not very smart. I should have gone with Andrew Smith to Hong Kong no matter what. If I did, I could stop to tell the story of my life but to conclude with a fairy-tale ending of "happily ever after."

There were a myriad of possibilities and options available. I could send Andrew Smith packing first. He could find a job and settle down in Hong Kong before I was ready to join him. He must be English. Many English people liked to work in Hong Kong, which was a British Crown colony. They held high positions, made good money, got housing subsidies, and many other staff benefits.

Instead of working for a paltry salary at a Canadian bank, Andrew Smith could easily find good jobs and get promotions like Charles Harrison, who rose to become the director of the department I worked in before I resigned.

By not going back with Andrew Smith to Hong Kong my fate was sealed. Perhaps in the grand scheme of things I was destined to fly solo on my journey in life, a journey to discover the real me. It was indeed very personal. However, wherever I went I always carried an extra piece of baggage, an albatross, which was my commitment to my siblings.

I told Madison about Andrew Smith's proposal to me. He did not say anything. He was not threatened because he somehow knew that if I was considering it, I would not mention it to him.

It was time for me to sponsor Heather over to Canada. She did not do well academically. She attended a vocational high school where she learned typing and sewing. She had been working as a typist back home for several months when I began her immigration process.

Meanwhile I resumed to live my life as normal as possible. In my leisure I listened to songs on the radio. The Beatles' "Here Comes the Sun" was very popular and it had a special meaning to me because it was summertime and my very first summer in Toronto. Other songs on the air wave included B.J. Thomas's "The Eyes of a New York Woman" and Jeannie C. Riley's "Harper Valley P.T.A." and later Tiny Tim's "Tiptoe Through the Tulips."

There was a big manufacturing plant that produced Canadian-style bread and buns in the midst of Chinatown. Sometimes the aroma of the onion buns drew me inside to get some freshly baked goods.

Madison was an avid sports fan. He liked American football especially. In the fall we went to a Canadian Football League game between the Ottawa Rough Riders and the Toronto Argonauts. His most favourite quarterback was Russell Jackson of the Ottawa

Rough Riders. The dominating American football quarterback was Joe Namath, nicknamed Broadway Joe.

On some weekends, Madison and I had dim sum lunches at the restaurants in Chinatown. They were not of the authentic types. There was no shrimp in the shrimp ball. There was only one good and expensive Chinese restaurant called Peking Palace in an affluent midtown neighbourhood. Their dim sum was the same as the ones back home. They even served scrumptious Peking duck. It was worth the extra money we paid.

Madison gave me his small black-and-white portable television. I watched "Mission Impossible" starring the husband-and-wife team Martin Landau and Barbara Bain. Michael Jackson was around ten years old when he performed on the TV show "The Jackson Five." "Rowan & Martin's Laugh-in" appeared on Friday nights, featuring the giggling Goldie Hawn, Lily Tomlin as Geraldine the telephone operator, and Arte Johnson as the German soldier.

Right after Christmas 1968 I came down with the flu. The flu season that winter hit us especially hard. It was called the Hong Kong flu, the mutated H3N2 strain. The middle-aged daughter of the then Governor General of Canada Roland Michener, died of it early the next year.

Since I worked at the Hong Kong government, I wanted to work at the government again. I applied for a stenographer position at the Ontario government and was hired. I quit the bank after working there for fifteen months.

Soon after I started my new job, Madison suggested that we should get married. He did not actually propose to me and I did not really care. I never had any warm and fuzzy feelings towards him. I asked him if there was love between us.

He replied, "Yes. We will be happy together." There was no mention of love whatsoever. He did not give me an engagement ring but I said yes anyway.

He seemed to be a decent man. He had a good job with reasonable pay even though he had to send money monthly also to support his parents in Hong Kong.

I understood clearly that according to what I had gathered from the old Chinese movies I saw, the oldest fatherless daughters who had to support their families would not get married until they had fulfilled their obligation, but I wanted to defy this way of thinking, which I found obsolete. I reflected on my relationship with Madison. With the way things were heading, Madison and I would end up getting married eventually. I would marry at a young age but I did not have to start a family right away and whenever I did, I would have two children, quit my job, stay home to raise a family, and be a full-time housewife. That was the plan.

Madison and I got married in August 1969, one month after the two first men, Neil Armstrong and Buzz Aldrin, walked on the moon. It was a small wedding in a Catholic church with none of our immediate families present. I walked down the aisle by myself. The wedding reception was held at Peking Palace. We invited Ethel, her whole family, and thirty friends to the reception. We had a big ten-course Chinese dinner, which we paid $10 per guest. That was the value of each wedding gift we received from our friends who were at the reception.

Following the wedding, Madison drove us to Niagara Falls, the honeymoon capital of Canada. We stayed there for two nights. Our next stop was Rochester, New York. At the border crossing in Niagara Falls, the American immigration officer looked at our passports. He asked us why we were entering the U.S.A. Madison told him the reason. The officer said to him, "You are old enough to be married but she is not." It is probably because I was not and I looked too young to get married.

We spent a few days in Rochester where we visited the George Eastman Kodak Museum. We got back to Toronto after being away for one week to start our married life.

At that time the use of birth control pills was prevalent but was not condoned by the Catholic church. My family doctor prescribed me with them. After I was on them for one month I had an empty feeling and it crept up once in a while. I had never felt that way before.

Two months later, Heather was ready to leave for Canada. I sent her the money to pay for the plane ticket. On her arrival in Toronto she stayed with us. I was busy assisting Heather to settle down and to look for jobs. Somehow the empty feelings disappeared.

Heather landed a typing position in an insurance company downtown. She was qualified to sponsor George to come as an immigrant. I did the same for David.

I suffered constant abdominal pain around that time. My family doctor sent me for tests. The result was I had gallstones, which were unusual for people my age. My gallbladder had to be removed. The surgery was scheduled for February the following year.

At the end of the year, Madison found a government job in Charlottetown, Prince Edward Island. He left Toronto right after the New Year. I was supposed to join him there after I had my operation. One week after Madison reported to his new position, he called me on the phone crying and told me that he was lonely and asked me to quit my job and fly to Charlottetown as soon as possible. He was the tenth child in a family of thirteen. He was not used to being alone, especially in a strange place. I was in Charlottetown a few days later. It was quite a change for me and Madison obviously. Prince Edward Island is the smallest province in Canada. Charlottetown is the provincial capital and the birthplace of confederation when the fathers of confederation gathered there first in September 1864, to plan the formation of the Dominion of Canada. It was named after Queen Charlotte, wife of George III of England.

There were no city buses because there was no demand for the sparsely populated city. We got around mostly by taxi if we did not own cars. Growing up in Hong Kong and having lived in Toronto for two years, I missed the hustle and bustle immensely.

Madison went back with me to Toronto for my operation in February. That was the first surgery I ever had and it went well. All of Madison's friends visited me at the hospital. They brought me flowers, which surrounded me. Most of them sat on the window-sill by my bed because there was not enough room to put them in the general ward I shared with three other patients. One of the nurses said that I was a princess.

I stayed in the hospital for thirteen days. After I was discharged, Madison went back to Charlottetown and I waited in Toronto for three more weeks for my follow-up appointment with the surgeon. I moved in with Heather after I left the hospital.

After I saw the surgeon for my follow-up appointment, I flew back to Charlottetown. I took a few more weeks to recuperate. While at home I watched television in the afternoon. The soap opera at that time was "Edge of Night" with Adam, Nicole, and Cookie as the main characters. I watched Adrienne Clarkson in "Take Thirty" on Canadian Broadcasting Corporation television. The cooking show on television was called "The Galloping Gourmet" with chef Graham Kerr and guest appearances of his wife, Treena. One day I heard on the local radio what fathers said to their sons then: "Son, there is more to life than joining the band."

When I felt well enough, I started working as a stenographer at a credit union, which was a subsidiary of the provincial government providing lending services to the local farmers, fishermen, and small venture entrepreneurs. The son of one of the Canadian inventors of insulin to treat diabetes, Banting and Best, had business dealings with us.

Madison made friends with some of the co-workers and a middle-aged Chinese man from Hong Kong who was a teacher at the city college. He invited us for dinner at his house. He lived with his wife and their two sons who were in their teens. There was a family-run Chinese restaurant where the chef/owner would cook authentic Chinese food for us.

When spring came we explored Prince Edward Island. There were lovely red sand beaches. We were at Cavendish where Lucy Maud Montgomery wrote *Anne of Green Gables*. We saw the play with Gracie Findlay as Anne at the Confederation Centre downtown. We loved the fresh lobsters, Malpeque oysters, scallops, and clams caught from the coasts along the Atlantic Ocean.

One of Madison's co-workers, an older man called Dennis, liked to play golf on the weekends. Sometimes Madison went with him to play on the nine-hole courses. I went with them occasionally. I did not play, but liked to walk with them and to help them retrieve golf balls that strayed into the woods.

One Friday evening, I went to shop at Kmart. I saw a young woman dressed in a light lime-green pantsuit like that of a nurse's uniform standing alone in the middle of the store. She hardly had any makeup on and had only an ordinary short hairdo. I looked at her and she looked at me. I did not know who she was. Two or three teenage girls stood a few feet in front of her and talked among themselves.

The following week, Dennis invited us for a concert by a female singer in a lounge bar. When the show began, a young lady with an egg-yolk-coloured long-sleeved blouse and a dark brown mini-skirt ran towards the stage barefooted, she was the young woman I saw in Kmart. She had a professional makeover and her hairdo looked very stylish. Her name was Anne Murray. I witnessed the performance of a rising star whose singing career took flight and soared higher and higher like the snowbird in her song which was written by a Prince Edward Islander, Gene MacLellan. Her brother, Bruce Murray, was also a singer.

Heather had a boyfriend in Hong Kong. Soon after she came to Canada, this boy wanted to break up with her, citing that his mother disapproved of her. She was distraught and became mad at me for deserting her when she needed me the most. She refused to talk to me when I phoned her. I was very upset that my sister and I were not on good terms anymore, but at the same time I felt pity for her. I knew she was hurt deeply.

On some weekends, Madison's co-workers invited us to their houses for drinks and snacks. I had wine, gin, rum, and vodka. I drank socially only. I did not like alcohol at all.

In those days I hardly heard of impaired driving and there were no seat belts in cars. When Madison and I went golfing with Dennis in his big General Motors car, Dennis was driving inebriated. Luckily we were not involved in any car accidents.

We went to the nearby Summerside Lobster Festival one summer weekend. I saw huge lobsters in fish tanks. National television personalities, Lloyd Robertson and Lorraine Thomson, were guests of honour.

During some weeknights, Madison went to harness racings. He liked to bet on horses. Once in a while I went along with him since there was nothing better to do.

The immigration visas for David and George were issued in the summer that year. They arrived in Toronto before school started. David just graduated from high school and George had one more year to complete. I paid the airfare for David and Heather paid for George, which was her way of paying me back for her plane ticket. My brothers brought Heather and me back together.

The three of them rented a flat on the second floor of a house from a Chinese couple who occupied the floor below. George enrolled in a high school close by. David did not have enough credits to be accepted into university. He went to a private high school in Peterborough, Ontario. I sent him $100 monthly to support him. Heather took over my turn to send money back home. There were only Mommy, Jane, and ah mah left behind in Hong Kong.

Near the end of the summer 1970, I started to feel not myself. I was not up to doing anything. I could not concentrate while at work. I was delirious when I described the symptoms to the doctor. I could not stop crying. He let me take a tranquillizer in his office. That was what he prescribed me to take at home. Valium was the common one at the time. His diagnosis was that I had severe agitated depression. A week after I saw the doctor I got back to my normal self.

On the weekends when Madison and I did not gather at his co-workers' homes, we went to movies. The movie that made a lot of buzz at that time was *Love Story* starring Ryan O'Neal and Ali MacGraw. Fran Tarkenton, an American football quarterback, cried while reading the book the movie was based on. It was written by Erich Segal.

I saw *2001: A Space Odyssey* directed by Stanley Kubrick and Thomas Hardy's *Far from the Madding Crowd* starring Julie Christie and Alan Bates.

After we were married, Madison and I opened a joint bank account. One day Madison was checking the bank statement and complained about the money I spent monthly to support my family, not that he did not have to do the same. The next day, I went to the bank to remove my name from the joint account and opened one solely for myself.

My mental depression recurred every month. On one of the visits with my doctor, Dr. MacDonald, I asked him if it had something to do with the birth control pills I was on. He replied that he did not think so but prescribed me with ones with lower dosage.

In the latter part of that year, the F.L.Q. in Quebec kidnapped the British diplomat James Cross, and the Quebec government labour minister, Pierre Laporte. They killed Pierre Laporte but released James Cross.

The new birth control pills I was taking did not seem to alleviate my depression. Dr. MacDonald suggested that I see a psychiatrist. He said it might open doors for me. He referred me to Dr. Hill. Before I began to talk, I asked him if my mental depression was caused by something physiological and not psychological. His answer was no.

He asked me all sorts of questions. I cried when I recounted my unpleasant childhood painfully. He said my father was a shadowy figure to me and he called him an alcoholic which was the first time I heard Papa being labelled as one. He asked if something was bothering me and I answered him honestly that there was none. The way he put the questions across made me tell him everything he wanted to know. I did not hold back anything. I poured out my soul to him. He wanted to know about my marriage and my life with Madison.

After seeing Dr. Hill for several weekly sessions alone, he wanted to see Madison and me together. He asked Madison a lot of questions about himself.

In the beginning of 1971, I was in a deep mental depression. My energy level was very low. I did not want to do or eat anything. I had suicidal thoughts. I dreaded leaving home to face the outside world.

I finally quit my job and when I told Dr. Hill about this he said, "You can still go on working but since you have already quit, make the best out of it."

I was bedridden. I slept twenty hours a day. Madison cooked dinners for us. He was a lousy cook and I did not have the appetite in the first place. There were not too many Chinese ingredients available in town to cook with anyway. The so-called Chinese nappa or cabbage was not of the real kind. It resembled the shape and taste of the cheapest Chinese vegetable, which Mommy bought sometimes. It was called *mother pig vegetable* because it was dirt cheap and it tasted bland.

One day Madison said to me, "A sick spouse affects the family life negatively." I did not say anything. He was not very understanding. Of course I knew that was the case. If I could help it, I would rather be healthy both physically and mentally.

My one wish while I was depressed was that I would feel better soon so I could cook for myself. Just to think of that I knew I had hope. I still had the will to live. I knew that when I came out of depression I would be back to my normal self, who embraced life the way porh pawh did.

I decided to stop taking the birth control pills and Dr. MacDonald introduced me to some other forms of contraceptive.

After months of seeing Dr. Hill, he informed me that I did not have to come soon and that Madison did not have to be present at the last session. When I was alone in Dr. Hill's office he went over a few minor things with me.

At the end of the visit, Dr. Hill concluded, "You are strong. Madison is weak. He never cries. If he gives you any hard time, give him a kick in the behind." I did not mention to Madison what Dr. Hill had said about him.

Dr. MacDonald and Dr. Hill played key roles in steering me to the right direction to battle my mental depression. I am forever grateful to them. Dr. MacDonald was right when he said that if I went to see a psychiatrist, he might open doors for me. Dr. Hill held that key for the doors. Up until then I had not mentioned my humble past to anyone. I was not shy in front of him. I did not feel any barrier between us. For once in my life I could open up to someone who cared to listen. I felt much relieved that I did not have to bottle up my humble beginning any more. A heavy weight had been lifted off my shoulder. It was cathartic.

Gradually I got back on my feet. I experienced depression periodically but it was not severe enough that I had to take tranquillizers. I tried my best to grapple with it drug free.

We had been married for two years in August 1971 and Madison suggested we should meet both sides of our family in Hong Kong. He had never been back home since he left in 1962. We arrived in Hong Kong in time for our second wedding anniversary.

We stayed with Madison's parents at their rental apartment. They were in their late sixties and were very old-fashioned. A few days later, Madison said to me that I had to say good morning to their parents every morning. I never had to do that to ah mah, porh pawh, or Mommy. I resisted and he said he wanted a divorce and would not be returning to Canada with me. I left his parents' apartment right away and went for a walk, thinking that I was a Catholic and was not supposed to divorce. I entered into holy matrimony reciting the vow, "in sickness or in health, for better or for worse, till death do we part." There was no grounds for divorce on such a trivial issue, so I went back to his parents' home. He did not take up the matter further with me.

On the way to my home in Wanchai on the second level, I was surrounded by a huge number of skyscrapers that went up after I left for Canada. Land was scarce in Hong Kong. In order to develop there was nowhere else to go but up. I looked up and I felt like a frog at the bottom of a well looking up at the sky. I was boxed in.

When I was at the Wanchai open market it was packed with shoppers. I almost had to rub shoulders with them. The population in Hong Kong kept on growing all these years I was away. There were around 4.5 million people who called this tiny British colony home.

It was an old Chinese tradition to visit their ancestors' graves one or two times a year. I went with Madison to his paternal grandparents' graves but he did not go with me to visit Papa's.

We took travellers cheques with us. Since I was not working, Madison paid for them. In the middle of our stay I ran out of money. We were at Mommy's home when I asked Madison for more money in porh pawh's presence. When she and I were alone later, she confronted me and said, "You asked your husband for money!!" I knew then she wanted me to be independent financially. I never asked Madison for pocket money again.

After three weeks we flew back to Charlottetown. Once back to work, Madison went on business trips to other Atlantic provinces. I accompanied him sometimes.

There were several male university students from Hong Kong attending the University of Prince Edward Island. Madison and I became their friends. When the Ping-Pong players from mainland China came to play at the University of Prince Edward Island, these students invited us to watch the game with them. These players' skill was superb. They played the ball back and forth with great speed and jumped up and down at the Ping-Pong table.

In the early 1970s, China wanted to open up to the outside world. Henry Kissinger went there to establish relationships between the U.S. and China. China sent their Ping-Pong teams to play overseas and it was called Ping-Pong diplomacy.

In the beginning of 1972, I felt I was well enough to go back to work. I found a temporary job to relieve someone on sick leave for six months. Mommy and Jane were still in Hong Kong. The immigrant visas I applied for them were approved.

I typed for a clerk who worked in a section of the premier's office. He was a kind old man. He told me to keep my cool, which made working for him stress free. My desk was right outside the premier's office. One day the premier stopped at my desk and talked to me.

One of the Chinese students from Hong Kong graduated from the University of Prince Edward Island that year. He invited us to the convocation. The premier's father, who was a former premier of the province, made a speech at the opening ceremony.

He began by telling us a joke, "A couple went to the convocation of their son who took algebra in university. The father asked his son to say something algebraic. His son replied by saying the symbol of the square root which his father mistook as 'pie are square.' He thought that he had paid a lot of money to send his son to university and on his graduation he did not expect to hear him say absurd things."

At the end of six months, I got another temporary position at another provincial government department. I was the assistant director's secretary. A middle-aged divorced lady from East Germany was the director's secretary. She had two young sons. She told me about her life in East Germany and that we had to be philosophical.

One evening George phoned me. At that time he was going to a university near Toronto. He said he was short of rent money and asked me to send him CDN$400. I did not have to pay for his airfare for Canada, so to make it up I gave him the money to pay his rent.

On the Thanksgiving long weekend that year, Madison drove me to Cape Breton, Nova Scotia, to see the changing colour of the maple leaves. While riding in the car, I looked out the window and saw a big stretch of green fields that made me think I would like living in a commune among the hippies. I envisioned it was a simple lifestyle, free of material possessions.

Madison became bored living in Prince Edward Island. His ultimate goal was to work for the federal government. He would have good job security, good pay, nice benefits, and longer annual holidays. He submitted an application to the federal government and was requested to go to Halifax for an interview. He was offered a position in a department in St. John's, Newfoundland.

By that time we had been married for three years and Madison thought it would be time for us to start a family and I agreed. Since most of my siblings were in Canada already, Mommy and Jane would be over soon, I no longer felt obligated to oversee their welfare. I was twenty-six years old and it was a good time for me to have children.

Before we moved to St. John's in the beginning of 1973, we went to Ottawa and Toronto for Christmas. We stayed with one of Madison's friends in Ottawa. That Sunday morning we went to mass at a Catholic school nearby. During homily the priest preached that parents should be firm, fair, and honest with their children. I told myself that this would be the way I would bring up my children.

In the beginning of 1973, we arrived in St. John's, Newfoundland. We resided in a hotel for two weeks. We ate at the hotel restaurant all this time. I heard Roberta Flack's "Killing Me Softly with His Song" frequently played in the dining room.

We moved out of the hotel into a rented newly built two-storey townhouse situated in the middle section of a hill in the suburb of St. John's. Newfoundland is larger in size compared to Prince Edward Island. When the Newfoundlanders mentioned west coast, they meant the west coast of Newfoundland and not that of Canada.

I found a typing position at a construction company. The office was located at the shopping mall near where I lived. One of my co-workers was the cousin of Gordon Pinsent, the Canadian film actor from Newfoundland. They had the radio on in the office and the popular song I heard at work was Helen Reddy's "Delta Dawn."

I typed specifications relating to the projects the construction company was working on. The bookkeeper of the company had to tally all the expenses on building materials and equipment weekly. It compiled several pages of tables all filled with figures. There were four typists in the office, but the bookkeeper wanted only me to type the reports every week. He told me that he liked my accurate typing.

Madison's office was in a federal government building by the St. John's harbour near the historical Signal Hill. On the weekends, one or two fishermen sold their catches on stands right by the harbourfront. We bought whole fresh halibuts for $1 a pound from them. I made bouillabaisse with them. There is a local Newfoundland dish called jig's dinner. It is made with corned beef, cabbage, and other vegetables. I cooked that once in a while. I found that lobsters from Newfoundland were not as tasty as those from Prince Edward Island. One time I cooked shark fish steak I bought near the St. John's harbour. I did not like its taste and texture. When we ate at restaurants we ordered cod tongues which is another local dish.

There was a marine laboratory near St. John's. We visited it a few times on the weekend. It overlooked the sea with icebergs floating in it.

One summer weekend, we took the ferry from Fortune, Newfoundland, to Saint-Pierre and Miquelon, a French territory off the southern coast of Newfoundland. French settlers who landed in Jacques Cartier's days in the sixteenth century came from Brittany, Normandy, and the Basque country. These French people kept the customs and traditions of their provinces and also their pure French language all through the centuries.

We stayed at a bed and breakfast place in a house in St. Pierre. We were served authentic French cooking. We strolled around the quiet town with 5,000 inhabitants. I bought baked goods at a French pastry shop. I shopped at a duty-free store to look for merchandise from Paris. I found two name-brand perfumes but could not decide on Chanel or Joy. I asked the salesperson for help. She recommended I should go for Joy. I paid CDN$20 for a bottle of Jean Patou Eau de Joy from Paris. I kept it as a souvenir and never opened it.

Mommy and Jane arrived in Toronto in the summer that year. Again, I paid for their plane tickets. They rented the second floor of a house owned by a Chinese couple. Jane attended the high school nearby. Ah mah was the only one left behind in Hong Kong. All our relatives were in Canada by then. She was in her early eighties. Because of her lifelong chronic cough, no nursing homes would take her in. Mommy finally found a Buddhist temple in the rural area of the New Territories where there were two rows of shoddy huts in squalid conditions on the ground adjacent to the temple. Ah mah was placed in one of these huts. She fared not that much better than the homeless people. Mommy paid a lump sum to the monks who oversaw the welfare of the tenants. When she died, she would be buried right beside the temple and not in the Catholic cemetery in Happy Valley as she had wished.

Mommy enrolled in English as a second language class. At the end of the course she found a job as an electronic component assembler at an electronic manufacturing factory. She was paid much more over the minimum wage and had good staff benefits. She finally landed a paid full-time job in her early fifties.

Madison did not find any people to play sports with in St. John's. He did not go to any horse races either because there was no racetrack around. We went to watch movies most weekends. Bruce Lee's kung fu movies were very popular then. I remembered *Enter the Dragon* particularly. The young men at my office liked his movies and talked about them often. Sadly his movie career came to an abrupt end with his sudden death in Hong Kong when he was in the prime of his life. My favourite movie I saw in St. John's was *Fiddler on the Roof*.

Madison watched almost all kinds of sports on television, NHL, CFL, NFL, golf, tennis, soccer, etc. We were one and a half hours ahead of Eastern Standard Time zone. That meant all these games were on later in St. John's. He also watched the national news on television every night at 11:30 p.m. I had to get up early to go to work so I went to bed ahead of him. That made it hard for me to conceive. I was finally pregnant after trying for almost one year.

It was a relatively easy pregnancy. I had morning sickness only if I had pizza or spaghetti the night before. So I stopped having Italian food. I craved potatoes and caplin, a small fish that looked and tasted like smelts. They were found along the shore in Newfoundland.

The instructor at the prenatal class was a midwife. She stressed the benefits of natural birth and I decided to follow her advice.

I stopped working at the beginning of the third trimester, thinking that was the end of my career as a typist. From then on I would stay home to raise a family.

Three weeks before the baby was due, Madison had to go to the west coast of Newfoundland on business for a few days. He drove his office car for the trip and I went with him. It took almost half a day to reach our destination, which was near Stephenville where we checked into a motel. That night we went to watch Marlon Brando's *Last Tango in Paris* in a tiny theatre.

I wanted Madison to be present at the time of my labour and delivery so he could see what I had to go through giving birth. We were in this together. I went into labour with a cold, one week before the due date. The whole process of natural birth relied immensely on breathing technique, but my breathing was hampered by my stuffed-up nose. The labour lasted twelve hours. Finally the nurse asked me if I wanted an analgesic. The pain was excruciating so I accepted her offer, but it hardly had time to work because I was ready to deliver. The pain was unbearable and I screamed shrilly. It seemed like an eternity before the baby was born. The obstetrician announced that it was a boy. Madison was happy because that was what he wanted. I would rather have a girl but when I took a look at the cute little newborn baby I did not care what the gender was. I was relieved that it was over and my breathing was back to normal immediately after I gave birth. The day I went home with the baby, Madison drove us home. I sat in the back with the baby in my arms. Back then baby car seats were not mandatory.

Taking care of a tiny baby was something new to me. There was a lot of work. Madison had to help with the housework, which he loathed. He complained that Mommy did not come to help us. I said to myself that I had to pay for Mommy's airfare to come over. If I did not plan to go back to work anymore I had to be careful with my money. I coped with the heavy workload myself without heaping too many chores on Madison to stop his grumbling.

We named our son Leonard and when he was two weeks old, Madison went to Ottawa, Ontario, for a job interview. He wanted to move back to Ontario. He applied for an internal transfer within the federal government. He would return home after the interview the same day. His flight was scheduled to arrive in St. John's late that night. I went ahead to bed and when I woke up a couple of hours to tend to Leonard there was no sign of Madison. I went back to bed and had a nightmare in which I saw Leonard lying on the floor outside his bedroom. He must have fallen from his crib and suffered injury. I was scared. When I got up early the next morning Madison was still not home. He did not phone me to let me know the reason for the delay. I became worried and called the airline company and found out from its recorded message that the plane had arrived. Then I called his secretary who told me that it was foggy the night before at the St. John's airport. The plane Madison was on was diverted to the Gander airport.

Soon Madison was notified that he got the job in Ottawa and was to assume his new position when Leonard was seven weeks old. We arrived in Ottawa, the nation's capital, in the middle of August 1974. It was around the time that Tom Cruise moved out of Ottawa. He attended school in the east end. His father was an engineer who had to move after several years on the job from one city to another.

We stayed in a utility motel in the west end for the first two weeks. One night Madison went with Gerry, one of his friends living in Ottawa, to the racetracks till very late. I was left alone with a tiny baby who kept on crying all night. I was very upset and I cried too.

Madison found a two-bedroom apartment near his office in the west end. I later found out that was where Paul Anka grew up and went to school. In the early 1960s in Hong Kong, I heard some of his songs such as "My Hometown", "Diana," and "Puppy Love" frequently. I passed by his former school sometimes.

The weekend before we moved into the apartment, Madison drove me and Leonard to Toronto to visit Mommy and my siblings. The next day Mommy babysat Leonard so Madison and I went to see *The Godfather II*.

Gradually we settled down in the new environment. I devoted all my time to being a housewife and mother. Madison socialized with his old friends who were working in Ottawa after graduating from the local universities. He played tennis and badminton with them on the weekends. Once in a while he went to the horse races with Gerry. When his friends invited us to have dinners at their houses, he did not want me to sit next to his male friends. He made me change seats with him.

Madison liked his government job. He dealt with paperwork related to the chemical field. There was no stress. After work he had a lot of time to lay back and relax.

When Leonard was nine months old, Madison suggested we should buy a house where there was more room for Leonard to grow up in. There were some brand-new townhouses near our apartment building which were within our price range and the down payment was low. We bought one with four bedrooms. We owned a house for the first time and it was a satisfying feeling, but we were soon disappointed because we had to park our car in front of our house on a driveway shared with the residents in the house attached to ours on the right side. There were four children ranging from six to twelve years old in that household. Their bicycles and toys were left on our side of the driveway and Madison was annoyed by it. He could not tolerate this so he put the house up for sale. It was sold after a couple of months. We hardly made any money from it since we lived there for only a short time.

That summer Heather got married in Toronto. She met her husband, Carl, two years her junior, through George who went to the same school with him in Hong Kong.

During the early months in Toronto, Mommy heard from ah mah once in a while. Ah mah, like porh pawh, was illiterate. When she saw students passing by her hut, she stopped and asked them to write to Mommy to tell her that she did not have enough to eat and that she was in a miserable state. Then there was no news from ah mah for a long time until around the latter part of 1976 when Mommy received a letter from the administrator of the Buddhist temple informing her of ah mah's death. She was cremated and the urn containing her ashes was kept in a small house beside the temple. Ah mah was eighty-six years old when she died, with no family members around her.

We moved into a new four-bedroom semi-detached house in the same neighbourhood in 1976. There was an attached garage and we had our own driveway. We took possession of the house the day before my thirtieth birthday. On my birthday, I was busy unpacking, cleaning, washing, arranging furniture, etc., and at the same time taking care of Leonard. It was not until exactly one week later it suddenly dawned on me that I had already turned thirty years old. I always feel that the twenty-nineth year of my life has been extended for one extra week.

Our new house was much nicer than the townhouse. It was more spacious and sat on a larger lot. Our neighbours who occupied the other side of the house attached to ours were very friendly. The husband, also a federal government employee, and the wife who had a home catalogue shopping business were middle-aged with two teenage sons.

With a bigger house came a bigger monthly mortgage payment and much more expenses to maintain the household. I found that to rely on only Madison's salary, there was hardly any money left-over from each of his pay cheques. It turned out also that his job was not as secure as he thought. There was talk of elimination of certain government jobs. In order to bring money home and not to have to sell our house in the event that Madison lost his job, I decided to go back to work.

My plan to have two children and be a full-time housewife was foiled. I would not have another child. Besides, there were too many starving children in other parts of the world. I could adopt a girl later on. Leonard went to a daycare centre when he was three years old and I started to look for a job.

I had a job interview at one of the largest chartered banks in Canada. When I arrived at the personnel office, there was a man sitting right close to the door. I told him what I was there for and that I had banking experience.

When I mentioned the name of the bank I worked at in Toronto, he said to me immediately, "Traitor!"

I later found out that man held a high position at one of the departments in the bank where I went for the interview. His name was Mr. Beaudry. I had to step past him to get into the bank. I took a typing and a mathematics test. The personnel manager told me there was a job opening at the main branch of the bank. It involved typing and taking incoming phone calls, which she was not sure if I was able to deal with. I needed the job desperately so I replied, "I am confident that I can handle it." She hired me and told me to report for work the next morning.

When I said to Heather before I came to Canada that I would go to all ten provinces to look for jobs if I had to, I did not go to all the provinces, but I had worked in British Columbia, the westernmost province; Newfoundland, the easternmost province; and Prince Edward Island and Ontario, the provinces in between.

I worked at the foreign exchange department in the bank. There was a lot of typing involved and part of it was for our cables section. I had to meet the deadline of 3 p.m. every day to hand over my work to that section, and one day the lady I typed for said to me, "Your typing is very accurate. You never make any mistakes."

One afternoon on my way to the cables section with the typed work, I passed by the desk of a clerk of another department and noticed that there was a note taped on the side of her filing cabinet which read, "You don't have to be crazy to work here but it helps." I then made a mental note that if working in the bank had driven me crazy, it was still all right.

The secretary of our manager, Mr. Boyd, was a young French-Canadian woman. Her name was Monique. She liked partying after work. When she got drunk and did not show up for work the next day, I had to replace her, which made my workload heavier.

After three months working at the bank, Mrs. Black, the personnel manager who hired me, got a transfer to another branch. One afternoon she came with her replacement, Mr. Henderson, to introduce him to the staff. When they were at my desk she said to Mr. Henderson, "When I asked Mr. Boyd about Marie's performance, he replied she was doing an excellent job. If he told me she was doing any better, I wouldn't believe him."

Through contact with customers on the phone, I soon learned some of them did not like to be asked direct questions even though they were not personal ones. So I had to be tactful and sometimes beat around the bush and ask probing questions.

Back in the late 1970s, all the banks closed their doors to the customers at 3 p.m. Monday to Thursday. Our supervisor, a French-Canadian lady, brought bottles of wine or liquor to work frequently and served them to us after the bank closed. One time one of the staff went to Mexico and brought back a bottle of tequila. We drank it straight. Its alcohol content was so high that they said it would kill the fly in the bottle.

After one year back to work, some of the symptoms of my mental depression appeared again. I found it hard to concentrate on my job. I could not afford to stay home when I felt depressed. If I took any sick leave, Monique would not do my typing, which had to be done daily. I also had a child to look after. I struggled to carry on as normal as possible. I did not mention it to Madison. We did not talk much anymore. I chose to suffer in silence.

I had kept a routine week in and week out since. It was a juggling act. From Mondays to Fridays I went to work. I took the bus to and from work. I spent three hours each day travelling. I left home early in the morning and came home late. I had to cook dinner and do the dishes. Then it was time for me to get ready for bed. I did not have time to tell Leonard any bedtime stories.

Ottawa is one of the few coldest capitals in the world. It was extremely cold when the wind chill was factored in. It dipped down to -49 degrees centigrade with the wind chill one morning on my way to work. The coldness went right to my rib bones through the two or three layers of woollen pullovers I wore under my heavy winter coat. It was brutal. We had a lot of snow too. On my way home from work at night I took a shortcut through a bicycle path. After a heavy snowfall, I dug my winter boots into the snow piled up to my knees. With the strong wind blowing on my face, I dredged myself in the dark alone. I felt like I was in Siberia. I had to battle the elements; rain, sleet, snow, or whatever mother nature threw my way.

On Saturdays, I spent the whole day planning and preparing meals for the coming week. On Sundays, I cleaned the house and ironed Madison's shirts. Sometimes I went shopping after work on Friday nights. I refrained from going when I felt depressed because it was impossible to make decisions.

Madison's job was not demanding. There was no deadline to meet. He could spend some time every morning reading newspapers or magazines. He had two coffee breaks and a long lunch hour every day. That was why he liked to have a job in the government.

Madison did not help me with any housework. The only thing he did inside the house was to give Leonard his bath at night. I did not have any time to handle any chores outside the house, so Madison mowed the lawn in the summer and shovelled snow in the winter. He had a lot of spare time, which he made full use of. During weeknights, he watched television for several hours until midnight. After dinner Friday nights, he went to the racetrack until the end of the last race. Some nights after the horse races, he went to the house of one of the Chinese men he met at the racetrack to play poker until early the next morning. After lunch Saturdays and Sundays, he went back to the racetrack and came home at dinnertime. On the weekends when the weather was warm, he played tennis with neighbours at the tennis court nearby in the morning before he went to the racetrack.

It was all work and no play for me. My only source of entertainment was again the good old reliable radio. It kept me company and it was hands-free, so I could work and watch over Leonard while listening to it. I found the Beach Boys "That's Why God Made the Radio" especially meaningful to me.

When Leonard was in the five years old kindergarten class, one of our neighbours babysat him before and after school. In the morning, I dropped him off at the babysitter's house before I went to work. Madison came home much earlier than me so he picked him up from the babysitter.

After work one evening when I was walking near home, I saw Leonard running out of the house. Madison was standing at the door and told me to run after him. I chased him down the street. He ran very fast. I could not catch up. I was out of breath and my heart began to ache. I turned back and went home. Madison started his car and I jumped in. He drove around the neighbourhood and finally spotted Leonard. He stopped the car and Leonard got in. I found out later that the two of them had an argument. Madison told Leonard to get out of the house and that was what he did.

I said to Madison, "Next time you tell Leonard to get out of the house, you run after him because I won't. It may give me a heart attack."

Aunt Betty, Uncle Bill, and Uncle Bob along with their families had immigrated to Canada and settled down in Vancouver in the 1970s. Porh pawh came with them. She alternated living with Uncle Bill and Uncle Bob. In her old age, she loved to watch wrestling on television. She never ceased to seek excitement, but my uncles were worried that it might be too much for her heart.

Porh pawh was eighty years old in 1980. I had not seen her since 1975 when she came to Toronto to attend Heather's wedding. I had two weeks of holiday that summer. Madison, Leonard, Mommy, and I went to visit her. We had an enjoyable family reunion. The day we left I gave her a hug. She was sad to see me leave. She cried because she knew that we might never meet again.

I struggled with my depression very hard. Honestly, I was tired of this awful feeling. I wanted to look for a solution to this dilemma. This had been going on for too long and I decided that it was time to find out its root cause. I started with keeping a chart of what I did and ate before I felt depressed. It took me no more than three months when I gathered that one or two days after I had alcoholic drinks at work, I felt depressed for about one week. I also discovered that caffeinated drinks would make me edgy. From then on I cut out alcohol and caffeinated drinks, and I was free of mental depression ever since. All the social drinking compounded with the birth control pills were the reason behind my severe mental depression. It is true you are what you eat, so I eat healthy now. At the same time I like to be close to nature whenever possible.

So far in my life I was very sensitive like Mommy who looked people in the eye to see if they disliked her to make her feel bad. I did not care what other people thought about me anymore. I did not want to be barely existing on earth or be a second-class citizen. As part of the verses of the poem "Desiderata" goes, "You are a child of the universe no less than the trees and the stars, you have a right to be here."

My self-confidence and self-esteem grew stronger every day. I became less sensitive and shy. I learned to assert myself at work. Gradually, I had emerged from a cocoon and transformed into an entirely different person.

After Jane finished high school in the late 1970s, she furthered her education at a university in Toronto. She majored in economics. After graduation she worked in a Japanese bank in Toronto. She had no steady boyfriend. Mrs. Chan, Heather's mother-in-law, had a nephew who was single and six years older than Jane. His name was Mark and was a professor at a university in Winnipeg. Mrs. Chan played matchmaker. She arranged for Mark and Jane to meet in Toronto. Mark came to Toronto periodically to go on dates with Jane.

George got married in June 1981. His wife, Olivia, was born in Canada of Japanese descent. Leonard was their ring bearer.

After working at the bank for a while, I found out that I had a good memory. My supervisor and co-workers knew that too. One afternoon, my supervisor was looking for the banking correspondent book to find out the former name of the Westpac Banking Corporation in Australia. Before doing that she said that I would know, which I did and told her it was the Bank of New South Wales.

Just before the bank closed early on Christmas Eve that year, our assistant manager, Denise, asked if I had seen a monthly government pension payment for a customer with the last name of McCoy. It was before the days of direct deposit. I typed up credit vouchers for the cheques for deposit into the customers' account.

Denise and the payment clerk searched them through and could not find it.

I had seen that name, but if no voucher was made up that meant the account number was not found and set aside in a pile. Denise checked that pile and found the "real" McCoy. She thanked me and wished me a merry Christmas.

In the spring of the following year, two men were sent to our bank for training. One of them was a young Englishman called Trevor. He stopped by frequently to chat with a young woman called Zeda working in our cables section. Trevor's father was the chief executive officer of a large international bank in Hong Kong. After a short time, they announced their engagement and moved to Hong Kong to be near Trevor's parents. This was another case of a young woman working in a Canadian bank where she was asked by an Englishman to go with him to work in Hong Kong.

One day in the early 1980s, Mommy heard from Aunt May that Mr. Lam in Seattle had died. After the Chinese restaurant he worked at as a chef closed late one night, he went to play mah-jong at a gambling house frequented by other cooks and waiters. The notorious Charles Ng got into the house and went on a shooting spree. Mr. Lam was among one of the dead. The killer fled to Alberta, Canada, and was captured later.

It was also around the early 1980s a U.S.A. space shuttle was scheduled to fly piggyback over Ottawa two times the same day, once in the morning and once in the afternoon. As I was walking towards the downtown bus stop with a co-worker after work, I heard a roaring sound overhead. My co-worker and I looked up and saw the space shuttle riding on top of a commercial airplane.

In April 1982, Queen Elizabeth II, accompanied by Prince Philip, came to Ottawa to sign the Canadian Charter of Rights and Freedoms into law. She did not visit Hong Kong when I lived there. I lined up near the Parliament Building to welcome them as their limousine passed by.

Mark and Jane planned to marry in 1983. Before their wedding, Madison, Leonard, and I spent a few days of holiday in Toronto. Madison's parents had already immigrated to Canada in 1974 and settled down in Toronto. Mommy invited all the in-laws over for dinner. When Mrs. Chan saw Madison's parents, she recognized them. Their family and Mark's family lived in the same apartment building in Hong Kong. Mrs. Chan's family lived in the building beside theirs. All their children were young then and the boys played soccer together in the courtyard in front of their buildings.

Jane moved to Winnipeg after the wedding. David wanted to buy a house and asked Mommy to live with him and contribute to the mortgage payments. She agreed with the arrangement.

Leonard started to listen to pop songs when he was nine years old. He liked Kool & the Gang, Boy George and the Culture Club, and Michael Jackson. He liked playing video games too. Madison bought him a Commodore computer in 1984. In January that same year, Apple introduced the Macintosh personal computer. At that time there was a saying that went "Commodore 64 eats the Apple core."

Our friends in Ottawa all owned single houses. I would have liked to own one also. I wanted to keep up with the Joneses. In the middle of 1980s, we bought a new four-bedroom single house.

Madison did not like to live in a large house, which meant more outdoor work. He showed his frustration and was in a foul mood most of the time. I tried to get out of his way, but sometimes I could not stand his meanness anymore and I talked back to him as Dr. Hill, the psychiatrist, told me to. Every time I did that I was reduced to tears. He said things that made me feel very small.

I worked across from Parliament Hill. One day in the early 1980s, I went out for a walk during lunch hour. I saw our prime minister, Pierre Elliott Trudeau, strolling by with a bodyguard behind him. The pedestrians did not bother to greet him. I looked at him and he looked at me and I walked away. It was a stark contrast to the time of Trudeaumania when I could not get near to hear him speak in Toronto in 1968. I regretted later that I did not talk to him when I had the chance.

On January 28, 1986, we were upset to hear that the space shuttle *Challenger* exploded soon after liftoff over the Florida coast. Seven crew members were killed.

A few months later, the telex machine operator/typist in the cables section went on maternity leave for ten months. Our assistant manager asked me if I wanted to be her relief. I would not be paid more money but I could learn new things. I accepted the offer. My duties involved mainly typing and sending money transfers and messages on the telex machine.

Shortly after I was at my new job, Mr. Boyd came to the telex machine room when I was alone.

He said, "If you don't like this job, come back to the foreign exchange department."

I replied, "I like what I am doing now."

He looked disappointed and left. The telex machine operator/typist decided not to return to work after her maternity leave and I got to keep the job.

My memory was put to test again at work one morning. Nancy, the clerk who was dealing with outgoing cable payments, was filling in details for wiring funds to a country in Africa that had recently undergone a name change. The list of wire charges had not been updated yet and it was still under that country's former name.

In order to look for the wire charges, Nancy asked out loud, "What was the name of that country before it was changed to Burkina Faso?"

I replied, "Upper Volta."

Several months later, Nancy's father, who held a senior manager position in the bank, retired. Nancy did not want to work in the bank anymore. After she handed in her resignation she said to me, "I have resigned. I want to break the news to you personally. I don't want you to hear it from somebody else."

In the morning of June 6, 1987, porh pawh lost consciousness at Uncle Bob's house. She had diabetes for many years. She was admitted to the hospital where she died that night. She was eighty-seven years old. Mommy went to Vancouver for the funeral. She retired one year before.

In October that same year, Madison's mother died in Toronto. She was eighty-one years old. Madison cried, which was unusual for him. I comforted him and he opened up and told me about his childhood. He had two older brothers and seven older sisters. Boys were highly regarded in the older Chinese families for they had to carry on the families' names. His father was a wealthy business-man but went bankrupt when he was ten years old. His mother gave birth to five of his older sisters consecutively before giving birth to him. When he was a small boy, his paternal grandmother gave him all her attention and kept him by her side. He was tied to her apron strings. His mother took him along wherever she went. His older sisters were jealous. They did not like the special treat-ment he got. They called him their mother's little purse. That made him feel very uneasy. The older girl who was born right before him bullied him a lot. I understood then why he was a male chauvin-ist and hated and belittled women, especially those like me who were not subservient. He took me as his older sisters, the bullies. I became his target to retaliate.

I was in the cables section for two years in 1988. My supervisor, Ruth, wanted me to be cross-trained in a clerical position that had nothing to do with typing. It dealt with collection. At the begin-ning of December that year, the collection clerk, Pat, fell on the icy driveway in front of her house and broke her right wrist. It had to be in a cast for six weeks. She was on sick leave. I had to relieve her. They hired two typists from a temporary employment agency to replace me. Agatha, one of the typists, was a middle-aged woman.

She was living in an affluent neighbourhood. She appeared to have her nose in the air. When I trained her, she did not pay much attention to me. Her body language gave me the impression that it was my fault that she had to work. Sandra, the other typist, was a young woman. She operated the telex machine. Her attitude towards me was the same as Agatha.

The collection function was centralized soon after I was on that job. Our branch had to handle collection for three other downtown branches. That was the work for more than one person. Besides, every day my in-basket was piled high with work that had to be emptied daily.

On the very first morning I was on the collection desk, Mr. Igusa from the embassy of a poor French-speaking African country phoned to inquire about the bank draft paid to his embassy by their government in Africa. The draft had to be cleared through our head office in Toronto. Mr. Igusa wanted to talk to a French-speaking person. There was a clerk who spoke French but she refused to talk to him because there was nothing to do with her. He and I communicated in English. Pat sent the draft to Toronto just before she went on sick leave. It took one month for an international transaction to be completed. I told him to call back and check, which he did at least two times a day.

For several days after I was on the relief desk, I worked feverishly before things got out of control. Finally Agatha could not stand it any longer to see the heavy workload I was subjected to.

She said to me, "Why don't you complain?"

I replied immediately without thinking, "I am too busy to complain."

By saying that I won Agatha over to my side. She said, "I'll never forget that you said 'I am too busy to complain.'"

Sandra began to treat me with respect too. Ruth knew she had to get another person to help me. She discussed it with her manager, Shirley, who had a friend looking for work. The next morning Shirley's friend, Becky, arrived. She watched what I was doing all day. The following morning Becky did not show up. She told Shirley that she did not like the job.

Shirley looked for someone within the bank to assist me. She found Amanda who happened to be the daughter of Mr. Beaudry, who was sitting at the door of the personnel office and called me a traitor. I had to step past him before I could step into the bank. Amanda took over the easy and simple tasks. After a few days on the job, she got a bad cold and stayed home for one week. Once again I was left on my own.

Around the middle of that December, another client, Mr. Chopra, who had a business account phoned and told me he was waiting for some documents from overseas sent to our branch via our Toronto head office. I called our Toronto office to trace it but they had not received it yet. Mr. Chopra phoned to check two or three times a week. Once in a while he came to our office to see me, which he was not allowed to do.

On December 21st, a bomb exploded aboard a Pan Am 747 plane over Lockerbie, Scotland. Two hundred and fifty-nine people on board died and eleven people perished on the ground. The U.S. Motown group, the Four Tops, was booked on that flight, but it was rescheduled, thus avoiding disaster.

As soon as the Christmas holiday was over, I called our Toronto head office to track Mr. Igusa's bank draft and Mr. Chopra's documents. The following day our Toronto head office called me back and told me that Mr. Igusa's draft had not been cleared and Mr. Chopra's documents were on board the ill-fated Pan Am jet. They would obtain duplicate copies for him.

Early in January 1989, Mr. Igusa's bank draft was cleared. I phoned him with the news and he asked me to go out for lunch that afternoon. I turned him down as he needed all the money he could get to run the embassy.

Mr. Chopra's documents arrived in my office in due course. When I handed the papers to him he was very grateful for what I had done for him.

At work one morning I was on a bathroom break. A secretary of the manager in another department was there too. We started talking. She said she wished that it was Friday when it was only Wednesday.

I replied, "I had the same thought this morning too but I asked myself, 'Is that how we are wishing our lives away?'" We both laughed.

She said, "My son has a Chinese friend who is a medical doctor. When my son got married this friend gave him $1,000 as a wedding gift. The Chinese people are very gracious."

Pat returned to work when her sick leave was over. I could not wait to go back to my typing job, but Ruth saw that I came through with flying colours, she had something bigger and better planned for me. She trained me on her job which dealt mainly with outgoing wire and telephone transfers for the whole branch. Some of these transfers involved huge amounts of money to be cabled overseas and had to be done before 12 p.m. our time. For telephone transfers for eastern Canada, calls had to be made before 3 p.m. our time, especially for transactions of large amounts since the furthermost province, Newfoundland and Labrador, was one and half hours ahead of us. For western Canada which was up to three hours behind us, I could make the calls right before I went home at 5 p.m.

After I was trained on Ruth's desk, she took sick leaves at least one or two days every month. The workload for that job was heavy. I had to grapple with the high volume of transfers and to act swiftly to meet the deadline.

Around the first half of that year, country after country in Europe discarded communism. The U.S.S.R. was known as

Russia. The Berlin Wall came down and East Berlin merged with West Berlin.

Young people and students in China joined in the action with no success and ended with the tragic June 4, 1989, Tiananmen Square incident.

At the French Open in tennis that followed, seventeen-year-old Michael Chang won the tournament for the U.S.A. He concluded his victory speech by saying, "God bless the Chinese people." The female champion at that tournament was another teenager, Arantxa Sanchez from Spain.

At that time, the popular song was Bobby McFerrin's "Don't Worry Be Happy." Whenever I was under pressure at work, I played that song in my head.

It was on the health news that doctors suggested we should laugh more often, which was good medicine. When I told that to Pat we began to take turns to make one another laugh.

There are many girls in our family. I do not need to adopt any. Heather has one son and two daughters. Olivia and Jane each have two daughters.

Near the end of that year, Ruth said to me, "There is an opening at the centralized word processing department. It will be a promotion for you. Do you want to be considered?"

I replied that I was interested. I got the job and I would assume my new position in one month.

There were two of us at the centralized word processing department. Charlotte was the other word processor. We got along well and supported one another, especially when we had to decipher the various officers' handwriting. One time Charlotte could not read the word "sound." She showed it to me but I could not figure it out. She said she would type in the word "solid." After a few minutes I realized that the word was "sound." Some time later, Charlotte asked for my help again. Someone wrote out the word "become" in such a way that we Chinese called that kind of handwriting "chicken intestine" because it looked crooked and all bunched up. Having read a few sentences I was able to tell.

Six months later the centralized word processing department was dismantled. I was transferred to the personal lending control department.

The work environment in my new department was more relaxed. The volume of my typing was much lighter and there was no deadline to meet.

On January 27, 1991, the day of the twenty-fifth Super Bowl in the U.S., Madison's brother-in-law called from Toronto to tell us Madison's father died that afternoon. He was admitted into the hospital after he fell at home a few days earlier. He died in his sleep. He was eighty-seven years old.

The Gulf War was on earlier that year when George Herbert Bush was the president of the U.S. and John Major was the British prime minister.

As the year went on, the Canadian economy sank into recession. Olympia and York, the real estate giant in Canada, declared bankruptcy.

In the summer, Mommy discovered a lump in her right armpit and needed surgery. It was removed and found not malignant. She stayed in the hospital overnight after the operation. Before she returned home, Jane's two daughters, Elizabeth and Rhoda, who were in Toronto for the summer holiday, helped me to hide Mommy's cigarettes and the lighter in a desk drawer in another bedroom.

When Mommy got back home I said to her, "Mommy, you have been smoking for decades, it's time to quit. If you smoke again, I will have nothing to do with you If you ever need help." She listened and never smoked again.

Later that year, the Canadian government began eliminating typist and word processor positions. Madison had to do his own word processing.

In 1992, my bank eliminated most of the typing positions. I lost my job and became a supernumerary. I reported to the vice-president's office. I worked at different departments that needed me.

Wherever I went that summer I heard Vanessa Williams' "Save the Best for Last" on the radio.

One Sunday afternoon that summer Mommy called me from Toronto.

She said, "David told me that he is gay. I phoned and told Jane and she said that I might not listen correctly. She told me to talk to him again. I did and he confirmed that was what he had said."

I realized then why I had the thought of homosexuality was natural when I was sixteen years old. It prepared me to deal with it later in my life.

I called David and I cried while telling him that I accepted him as he was.

He replied, "I am happy at least one sibling does not reject me."

No other family member wanted to have anything to do with him anymore.

One day, Jane and Elizabeth were walking in front of David's house. Elizabeth, who was six years old at the time, said to Jane, "Mom, I want to stop for a minute to look at the house." She had stayed in that house every time she came to Toronto since she was a baby.

She asked Jane, "What had happened to Uncle David? Did he die?"

Jane did not answer.

Heather did not want Carl to know, but he soon found out when he met David on the street and he told him about it. Gregory, Carl and Heather's son, two years younger than Leonard, was with Carl at that time. Heather, George, and Jane did not want any of their children to know about their uncle's sexual orientation. George's way of reasoning was that when his two daughters grew up he did not want them to follow David's footsteps and become lesbians. Anyway, Gregory knew and he later told his two younger sisters, Dorothy and Emma.

David picked the worst time to come out of the closet. AIDs was running rampant. *Time* magazine featured an article on this subject that summer. I bought a copy.

I talked to George to persuade him that a homosexual was born that way and not by choice, but he did not listen to me.

George said, "I refuse to shake hands with faggots."

Heather and Jane did not want anything to do with people who were gay either. One day Carl told Heather that he knew what had happened and asked her why she did not tell him, but she said she did not know. Jane decided to keep it as a secret from Mark. I told Madison and he did not want me to tell Leonard. He reasoned the same way as George.

A couple of things of interest mentioned in that featured article in *Time* magazine were that a doctor of Asian descent in the U.S. was working on drugs for AIDs and that many boys in their late teens were gay. I mentioned it to Leonard but he said it was a media sensation.

I understood that the daunting task of reuniting David with the rest of the family fell on me. I had to find a way, although at that time it seemed mission impossible.

In the spring of 1993, the bank recreated the typing position in the loan processing department and I got the job back. I looked forward to going to work every morning with a happy and satisfying feeling.

David put his house up for sale. It was sold in a few months. The proceeds were divided between him and Mommy. Mommy's share amounted to $75,000 and David kept $95,000.

I suggested to Mommy that she should buy a condominium apartment with the money. It might not be enough to cover the total price, but I had savings and I could pay for the difference.

Mommy started searching for resale apartments, which were more affordable than the brand-new ones. The pre-owned ones did not appeal to her. She found they were old. She decided to rent instead. She said that we all lived in nice and modern houses. She wanted to rent a new, luxurious one-bedroom apartment for one year. She found one with a monthly rent of $1,000.

She divided the money she had among her five children. She gave Jane $30,000 because she paid the household expenses while living with her for years. She gave the rest of us $10,000 each. Since she did not want to see David anymore, she asked me to hold onto his share until he had a need for it.

I called David to find out if he intended to buy an apartment unit. He said, "Apartments do not sit on land. They don't have much value." He preferred to rent and he found a one-bedroom apartment midtown.

Leonard graduated from high school in the summer of 1993 and was accepted into one of the universities in Ottawa. I was pleased that he decided to further his education so he would have a brighter future.

On the last Saturday evening in October that year, we were invited for dinner at our neighbour's house. Leonard went to a party at the university. Madison came home from the racetrack just before the dinner date. I had been busy working in the kitchen all day and was not ready. He stood by the front door to wait for me. He had a red jacket on and a ready-to-kill look on his face. As I was running upstairs to get ready, I told him it would take a little while. He did not like to be late and tried to hurry me. I said I was not going.

He replied, "I'm not going either. I want a divorce."

I cried and the floodgate opened. If it was not Saturday night I would not do that because I did not want to go to work the next morning with swollen eyelids.

We had a joint staff bank account with no banking service charges. I looked for his client's card and credit card at my bank and put them away.

He went into the bedroom after a while and said, "I did not show respect even to my father. I scolded him when I wanted."

I said, "You are not human."

I went to bed early that night without a bite to eat. I cried myself to sleep. The next morning I cooked a big breakfast for Leonard and myself.

I waited for Madison to bring up the subject of divorce again. While I was home after work in the middle of the week, Madison said that he went to the bank and found that his client's card was gone and could not do any banking. I knew all the privileges of having a joint staff bank account would deter him from divorcing me. Later that night I put the cards back in his wallet.

In the spring of 1994, our loan processing functions in Ottawa and area branches were centralized. All the departments involved were moved into an operation centre in the southern part of the city. The brother-in-law of one of my co-workers who sat beside me was a Hollywood movie director.

One afternoon, three or four of my female co-workers gathered near my desk. They talked about not coming back as women in their next life.

I said, "I'm not coming back period."

Sophie, one of the young co-workers, shouted, "Marie!"

I smiled.

Having lived in a trendy apartment for almost a year, Mommy thought of moving because she could not afford the expensive rents any more.

I said to her, "There are brand-new condominium apartments for sale. They may not be located in ideal neighbourhoods, but they are more affordable. Start looking and if you find some suitable ones, let me know. I have some savings now. I will buy one for you if it is within my price range."

After a month, Mommy told me she found a new one-bedroom apartment in the east end. I took a week of holiday and went to Toronto alone. Mommy and I went to check out the place. It was bright and spacious.

The next day we went to the sales office at the apartment building and bought a unit. There was a big supermarket in the shopping mall nearby. We went inside the mall and shopped for a while.

The following morning, Mommy sat in the living room looking upset. I asked her what the matter was. She said, "There are too many ethnic groups around the neighbourhood I'll move into. I feel uneasy among them. I will go to live with Jane in Winnipeg for one year."

It was typical of Mommy who planned her future one year at a time.

I said, "When you come back from Winnipeg after one year, where will you live? If you end up homeless, I won't come to your rescue. Let's go to the apartment building and have another look." I had to talk some sense into her.

When we were there, we stood outside to observe for a while. We saw a few Chinese people going in and out, and a young Chinese woman in a nice car parked in front of it. If other Chinese people could live there, Mommy could too.

I said to her, "I will phone the police department to check what the neighbourhood is like."

The policeman I talked to said, "It is a safe neighbourhood for your mother. It is safe everywhere in Toronto." This put her mind at ease.

I went to Toronto during Chinese New Year 1995 to help Mommy move. She paid the monthly condominium fee and I paid the property taxes. We had Chinese New Year dinner in the new apartment while I was watching the American Super Bowl football game on television. The San Francisco 49ers with Joe Montana as their quarterback won the game.

In the spring of that year, Mark, Jane's husband, applied for a position at one of the largest universities in Hong Kong and got a job offer he could not refuse. He would be the head of a faculty department with a salary many times that of what he was earning in Canada.

Later that summer, Jane moved back to Hong Kong with Mark and their two daughters. After they had settled down in their new home, Mommy went before Christmas to see them in Hong Kong.

We planned to go to Toronto for Christmas and could have Mommy's apartment all to ourselves. One week before Christmas, Madison got a cold and I caught it from him a few days later. We left for Toronto on Christmas Eve. When we arrived, Madison parked his car in the underground garage. I took some bags and went ahead to the elevator. While I was waiting for the elevator, I heard a heated argument between Madison and Leonard. Madison must have said something aggravating to Leonard who said, "I have been doing well in university and now you said I am no good. It made me feel down."

The elevator door opened at that moment and Leonard stepped immediately inside, closed the door, and went up alone. When we were up at Mommy's apartment there was no sign of Leonard. He left the bags behind and disappeared. When I thought of what he said about feeling down, I feared for the worst. There were nine floors in that building. I got outside as soon as I could, walked around the building, looked up the roof to see if Leonard might try to jump down. I did not see him up there. The next place to look would be the nearby shopping mall. I was sick and it was a cold and wintry day, which made me feel more miserable. I did not know if I could ever find Leonard. It is a big world, but I would not give up.

When I was inside the mall, the first place I went to was the record store Leonard frequented. He was not there. I saw one or two young men with the same winter coats Leonard was wearing. I walked near them and it was not him. There were two more places I could check out: the Consumers' Distributing Company where customers ordered merchandise from the catalogue and McDonald's restaurant. I went into the Consumers' Distributing Company first. I stood behind the customers who were placing their orders at the counter. I looked at each one of them carefully. All of a sudden I felt a hand on my shoulder. I looked back and saw Leonard. I was relieved. I could celebrate Christmas joyfully with Leonard back with me.

As a birthday gift from me to myself for my fiftieth birthday in 1996, I wanted to go to Hong Kong on my holiday. It was my wish to return to my birthplace before the handover to China in 1997. As a side trip I would go to Brisbane, Australia, to visit Catherine, whom I last saw in 1962. On my way to Hong Kong I would stop over in Vancouver to see Uncle Bill, Uncle Bob, and Aunt May. Uncle Simon died in 1993. Aunt Betty went to visit Mommy that summer. I would take the whole month of November off. I asked Madison to come along but he declined. He bought me a suitcase on wheels for my trip.

I began my holiday soon after my fiftieth birthday. My first stop was Vancouver. Uncle Bill and Uncle Bob were thrilled to see me. I stayed with Aunt Betty for a few days. The night before I left for Hong Kong, Aunt Betty asked me about David. She told me when she was in Toronto earlier she tried to find out from Mommy. She said whenever Mommy opened her address book, she would peep over it to look for David's address and phone number. She knew that Mommy would not tell her anything if she asked her. I cried while relaying David's story to her. She said Mommy and my siblings should not treat David that way. I gave David's phone number to her.

The new runway at the Vancouver International Airport opened the day I left for Hong Kong. As my flight was approaching Hong Kong, I watched the news on the in-flight television and heard that a plane was missing in Nigeria.

I arrived in Hong Kong safely. I stayed with Jane and her family. The first place in Hong Kong I wanted to go back to was the house I grew up in. It was torn down in 1972 and was replaced by a condominium apartment building. I stood in front of it and started to reminisce. I saw the thirteen old stone steps leading to the entrance of my old apartment were still there for sentimental reasons. It was nostalgic. The next stop was the Italian convent school I attended. It looked the same with a new extension next to it.

One morning Jane took me to Sha-tin, which used to be a countryside. When I was in high school, we went there for school picnics. It was well developed with many tall condominium apartment buildings and large shopping centres.

Jane and I went to the Buddhist temple where the urn with ah mah's ashes was kept. The two rows of dilapidated huts were still there. I looked inside them and found each one was occupied by a single old lady. It was a shabby place for ah mah to spend the last few years of her life on earth in solitude.

I was in Hong Kong for about one week when I heard on the news that an airplane sitting on the tarmac in one of the major airports in India caught fire.

On November 20, the sixteen-storey Garley commercial building in Kowloon was on fire. There was no sprinkler system inside. Horrified office workers on the upper floors were trapped and screaming for help. Forty-one people died and eighty-one people were injured.

I arrived in Brisbane near the end of the month. I was overjoyed to see Catherine again and to meet her husband, Isaac, who was a dental surgeon and the direct descendant of Confucius. They have three daughters. The two younger daughters are twins born one month before Leonard.

I stayed with Catherine in her big house. We went to a koala bear sanctuary and had my picture taken with a koala bear. The then U.S. President Bill Clinton was in Australia at the same time for the Asia-Pacific Economic Cooperation Summit. He had his picture taken with a koala bear also.

Catherine drove me to nearby Radcliffe, where the Gibb brothers of the Bee Gees lived before they moved back to England.

One morning I saw in the headline of a local newspaper that a plane crashed off the coast of Ivory Coast. Since the beginning of that year, plane crashes occurred almost every second month. 1996 is the year of the worst aviation disasters on record.

I flew back to Ottawa after staying in Brisbane for one week. I arrived home safe and sound.

On July 1, 1997, the handover of Hong Kong back to China took place amid pouring rain at the Hong Kong Convention Centre. I watched the ceremony on television. It was attended by Prince Charles, the then British Prime Minister Tony Blair, the last governor of Hong Kong Chris Patten, and some high-ranking Chinese officials. Chris Patten and his family boarded the royal yacht *Britannia* and sailed away from Hong Kong to Singapore where they disembarked. The song "Rhythm of My Heart" composed by Marc Jordan was played.

Later that summer it was announced that the operation centre would be closed early in the following year. We had to look for another job within the bank ourselves. One morning Nora, one of my co-workers, told me about an opening on the bank job posting site, which suited me. Nora came from the Channel Islands and she lived near me. Sometimes we took the same bus to work.

I applied for that position but I did not get it. Another typist who had only a few years of banking experience was the successful candidate.

I was on my holidays in August. One day at home I suddenly thought that I had not played John Denver's tapes for two decades. I had a strong urge to listen to them and that was what I did.

In October we went to Toronto for Thanksgiving. On the way home on October 12th, I heard in the news on the car radio that John Denver died in a plane crash he piloted himself off the coast of California. I wondered if that was a coincidence or a premonition when I thought of listening to his songs just two months earlier.

I found a teller position at one of the branches near the end of the year. It was located in a poor part of the city where prostitutes and drug addicts hung around. When I told Madison about it, he said, "You can't do it." He knew tellers served all kinds of customers. Some of them were difficult to deal with. Madison thought I was as sensitive as he was, it was not a suitable job for me. He did not know I was no longer sensitive. If I worked for four more years I could retire early at fifty-five years old.

When I was in Toronto for Christmas that year, Mommy told me an unpleasant experience she had at her bank. She said, "I handed my bank book to the teller and she asked me if I wanted it updated?"

She was offended by being asked such a question. She rebuked, "If I don't want it updated, why would I hand it to you."

I said to her, "I will be a teller soon. If you don't want your daughter to have nasty customers, remember to be nice to them."

Right after the new year 1998, I started my training in a downtown branch. There was a very nice and experienced teller trainer at the main branch. Her name was Ruby. She was suffering from a hard to cure disease and was on long-term disability at that time. Somehow I wished I could have her to be my trainer.

On the first day of the training, freezing rain began to fall. The sidewalks were coated with ice. I had to slip and slide all the way. After I was inside the bank for a short time, my trainer showed up. To my surprise it was Ruby. It was a dream came true. She was back to work temporarily at the request of the human resource officer to train me for three weeks.

The freezing rain continued falling day and night since Monday in Ottawa and as far east as Montreal. At one point, some nearby major highways became so slippery they were littered with stalled cars and trucks.

For at least two mornings there was no electricity in my branch, which was forced to close until the power came back on in the afternoon.

On Thursday afternoon, the electricity was out and the freezing rain was still falling relentlessly. It crippled the whole city. Office workers were sent home and were told not to come back until the following Monday. We were hit by an ice storm which lasted for almost one week. I had never heard of such a storm and I thought it must be a once-in-a-lifetime experience.

After my three weeks' training, I reported to my new branch. I worked in the frontline serving customers all the time. I met all kinds of people. Before closing time one day, I was serving a Mr. Nash who dated his credit voucher 1992. I had to point that out to him and asked jokingly, "Where were you all these years, Mr. Nash?" We both laughed. I had learned to flirt.

The popular song at that time was Toni Braxton's "How Could An Angel Break My Heart."

All my new co-workers were nice to me. Two of them, Carmela and Ada, were extremely kind. Carmela came from Italy and she said people told her she looked like Gina Lollobrigida, which was true. Ada came from Scotland and she was the tellers' supervisor. Mr. Beaudry's son, Stephan, also worked at that branch. So I ended up working with all the children of Mr. Beaudry, the one who called me a traitor.

One day Ada said to me that she and Carmela had dinner with Nora. The three of them had worked together before. I realized then Nora had put in a good word for me. I was grateful to her but did not have the opportunity to thank her in person.

Leonard graduated from university in the spring. He found a job in Toronto. His high school classmate Will Shiu was also a teller in my branch.

In the summer of 1999, my friends Bryna, Corinne, and I went to see *The Sixth Sense*.

We ate at a restaurant before the movie. During lunch we heard the news that a Taiwanese airline plane flipped over while landing in the midst of a typhoon at the new Chek Lap Kok International Airport in Hong Kong. Three people were killed. The pilot was Italian.

That same year, Madison and I went to Toronto for our holiday. One evening Mommy invited George and his family for dinner at her apartment. I wanted to talk to George about David again. I asked Madison beforehand to help me change George's mind. He respected him. During dinner I brought up the subject. Madison kept mum. George did not want to listen and lost his temper. Although we spoke in Chinese, which Olivia, Thelma, and Irene did not understand but could sense what we were talking about. George left with them as soon as dinner was over.

When I was alone with Mommy the next day, I mentioned the same subject to her. She did not like to listen and turned her head so as not to face me.

She said, "I do not want any gay man to be my son."

I felt very upset. I thought she was worse than animals, which would not abandon their offspring they gave lives to. George called later that day to apologize for what he did the night before. He said he was not ready to accept David yet, but he might change his mind in time.

I replied, "You have your own family to think of and I understand."

Later that year, Mommy had a severe heart problem. She was admitted to the hospital intermittently. Finally her family doctor told George that her condition had deteriorated and in the worst-case scenario she had only a thirty percent chance of survival.

I remembered that Mark's friend, Dr. Wong, was a cardiologist in Ottawa. I called him and told him about Mommy's condition. He gave me the diagnosis according to what I had told him on the phone.

I asked, "If my mom comes to Ottawa, can you see her?" He said he could. George came with Mommy to see him. He told us there were two solutions. One was valve transplant, which was risky. The other was angioplasty, which might be good for only two years.

We did not know what to do. Mommy could decide for herself.

I said to her, "Mommy, you like gambling. What would you like to do?"

Mommy thought for a minute and replied, "I want a transplant."

Dr. Wong referred her to a well-known heart surgeon, Dr. Wilkinson, who sent Mommy for scans that showed she did not only have two diseased valves but also one blocked artery, which required a bypass. Mommy needed an open-heart surgery. The valves would be replaced by carbonated steel called the St. Jude's valves. She was placed on a waiting list unless her condition had worsened, then she would have an emergency surgery. Mommy stayed in my house to wait for the operation. Madison did not like to live with her and showed his disgruntlement to me. I kept quiet to avoid any confrontation with him, especially not in front of Mommy who did not like to live with us anyway.

In the meantime, Mark bought a new three-bedroom condominium apartment in uptown Toronto for him and his family to stay whenever they came for visits. It was ready for occupancy in September that year. Since Mommy's heart condition had stabilized, she went back to Toronto and moved into Mark's new apartment.

I told David about Mommy's heart problem and he wanted to see her right away. I knew she was not ready to see him so I told him to wait until after the surgery.

Soon after Mommy left Ottawa, Madison said to me, "I want a divorce so you can take care of your mother full-time." I thought he was foolish and ignored him.

He said, "You and Leonard drove me to gamble."

I retorted, "What did you say? You started gambling when Leonard was only a baby. How could he do such a thing?" He had nothing more to say.

Mommy's surgery was scheduled just before Christmas. A co-worker's father-in-law also had the same kind of operation by Dr. Wilkinson one month before Mommy's.

Soon after we found out when the surgery would take place, I heard on the news that Dr. Wilkinson approached an undercover prostitute on his way home one night. He was sent to John school. All his scheduled surgeries were put on hold.

At the end of 1999, we were eagerly anticipating the arrival of the new millennium. There was a lot of talk of Y2K and was uncertain when the moment we rang in the year 2000, there might be glitches on things that ran on computers. When I woke up on New Year's Day, I found all the hype was needless.

At the beginning of the new year Mommy's surgery was scheduled at the end of February.

Jane came to Ottawa to be with Mommy. The morning of the surgery, Jane and I were assigned a waiting room. Around noon-time, Dr. Wilkinson appeared and told us the surgery was over. Mommy lost a lot of blood and needed a blood transfusion, but she would be all right. We went to see her in the intensive care unit later that afternoon. Everything seemed fine so we went home.

We were still in bed around 5 a.m. the next morning, a nurse from the hospital phoned and told us Mommy's blood pressure was very high and she was in critical condition. Before we left for the hospital, the nurse called again and told us that Mommy's condition had been upgraded to serious. She had to go for another surgery. We sat quietly in the waiting room all morning until the head nurse came. She said the surgeon had to open Mommy up again. A specialist was consulted and he suggested that nothing more needed to be done. Mommy was stitched up so as to prevent any infection if her body was being exposed for too long.

We went to see Mommy when she was in the intensive care unit. Her face was puffy. Her attending physician came in and said that he could only tell her condition hour by hour.

At 8 p.m. that night, I stood by the waiting room door and saw Dr. Wilkinson. He stopped and said, "Your mom is okay." Coming right from Dr. Wilkinson, I was assured that Mommy was out of danger.

Mommy was released from the hospital ten days after the operation. Jane went back to Hong Kong after Mommy had her surgery. Mommy went to see Dr. Wilkinson for the follow-up appointment three weeks after she was discharged from the hospital. He said that everything was all right and prescribed her with medications for her heart.

Mommy stayed in a long-term care home in Toronto to recuperate. It took her a long time to recover but eventually regained her strength and her quality of life did not have to suffer.

That summer Aunt Betty and Uncle Harold came to Toronto to see Mommy and stayed with her for two weeks. I was in Toronto for a few days to meet them and took them to visit David. I mentioned to Uncle Harold that as soon as I found a job in Toronto in 1968, I sent home an extra CDN$10 every month to repay him for my plane ticket. He said Mommy never gave him the money. To make up for it, I treated him and Aunt Betty with a three-day bus tour among the tourist attractions in Ontario.

Bryna, Corinne, and I met for lunch that year. The following day a plane plunged down into a residential area soon after take-off from one of the airports in New York City.

I was in Toronto for Christmas. I told Mommy that David wanted to see her. She agreed since she realized she was granted a new lease on life and should take on a different viewpoint on things. They were happy to be reunited.

In September 2000, Pierre Elliott Trudeau died. He was to lie in state inside the Parliament Building. I wanted to go and pay my final respects to him but many people from other cities came too. The lineup was very long, so I did not go but watched documentaries about him on television the day before the funeral.

At the end of 2000, I decided to retire in 2002 and moved to Toronto to be near Leonard. Madison wanted to retire at the same time. There was a condominium apartment project about to be under construction right beside Mommy's building. I liked the location so we bought a two-bedroom unit, which would be ready for occupancy in time when we retired.

Heather's older daughter, Dorothy, was attending a university in downtown Toronto in the early 2000s. She rented a room close to the university. I was in Toronto on my holiday and I invited David for dinner downtown. On our way to the restaurant we passed by Dorothy's house. David wanted to check if Dorothy was home but she was not. On the way home we passed by that house again and David knocked on the door. Dorothy was there this time. When she saw David she ran over to him and gave him a big hug. It was a moving scene. Dorothy told Heather later that she had seen David. Heather realized that she should not turn her back against her brother and started to see him again.

After the new year 2001, I thought only of my forthcoming retirement. That made me feel anxious and gloomy until the morning of September 11. On my way to work, I passed by the federal government headquarters. The public workers were on strike at that time. They sat outside the buildings and had the radio on. I did not pay any attention to the broadcasting. I took a shortcut by going through a shopping mall. Once inside there was a large crowd gathering in front of a television in a dental office. I saw both the twin towers at the World Trade Center were on fire. Some people said that two planes flew into the top of the towers. We later heard about what had happened to the Pentagon and the plane crash in Pennsylvania.

I watched the comprehensive coverage of the news on television all evening. The streets of Manhattan were packed with pedestrians covered with dust and running for the Brooklyn Bridge. Before the twin towers came tumbling down, a young woman knelt down on the sidewalk with tears in her eyes as she watched a man and a woman jumping down from the top of one of the burning towers to their death.

Thirty-plus flights on their way to the U.S. were diverted to the Gander International Airport in Newfoundland. Their local community centres and residents opened their doors to the several thousands of stranded airline passengers who were touched by this outpouring of humanity.

The world was forever changed from that day on. We were told to keep our eyes and ears open. I now try to stay alert constantly.

In February 2002, we put our house up for sale. Our real estate agent, Winona, was very experienced. It was still winter so there were not many activities in the housing market. When spring came our house was not sold yet and Madison wanted the asking price lowered. More prospective buyers showed up but there was no offer. Madison became very impatient and was in a foul mood. He liked to rant about why our house took so long to be sold before he went to the racetrack every Sunday.

In early April, two weeks after our asking price was lowered, Madison wanted to have the price reduced again. While he was out playing Ping-Pong one evening, Winona phoned to make her weekly follow-up call. I told her about Madison's intention.

She asked me, "What do you think?"

I replied, "If the price has gone down any further, I feel like I am giving my house away."

Winona said, "Let me handle this. I will talk to Madison tomorrow."

She talked him out of it.

On my way home from work one late afternoon near the end of April, I met Winona in front of my house. She told me someone came to look at our house that morning. After dinner that night, Winona phoned to tell us that there was an offer from that someone but it was a shaky offer.

After one week the offer became firm. The closing date was mid-June, two weeks into my retirement. I had wished that I could spend some leisurely time in my single house after I retired. I never got around to doing it while I was working, but I did not have such luck.

The construction of our apartment building was completed ahead of schedule and was ready for occupancy soon after we moved out of our house. The day we moved out of our house, Madison felt so elated that he hugged my back as he was standing behind me, but I did not turn around to hug him back.

Soon after I began my retirement, I heard on the news that the baby boomers had reached their final frontier. They wanted to grow old gracefully. That was what I had intended to do although it was easier said than done for my retirement did not have a good start. It would be a challenge to live with Madison full-time for the first time. He would drive me crazy and make me run up and down the street like a chicken without a head.

Our apartment measured 950 square feet. It was not big. One day Madison was in the living room and I was standing in the foyer. He said to me, "Come near. I have to talk to you." I could hear him without going over to him. I did as he said so as not to make a fuss.

One day I found out there were discrepancies in our utility bills and property tax statements. I checked with Madison early the following morning. He said to me grumpily, "You have made my day." I then realized that he stayed up late every night and did not have enough sleep, he hated to deal with problems in the morning.

Madison did not like to stay home all day long. He played badminton and tennis in the mornings. He went to the racetrack in the afternoon two times a week and bet on horses online at home every day.

After dinner I watched television. One night the sequel to the movie *Love Story* was on. Ryan O'Neal reprised the role and Candice Bergen played against him. I watched only the scene when the two of them were in Hong Kong.

I started to write notes to Madison on anything that I needed to discuss with him. I talked to him only later in the day on things that were too lengthy to put in writing. One afternoon he said something to me and I answered, "Okay." After hearing this, he said, "People may think you sounded annoyed."

I said in English without thinking, "I live my life the way I want, not the way people want me to."

He said, "Why did you answer me in English?" I did not tell him why but I did not know how to put the words in Chinese right away.

Every time I began to say something, he did not like to hear it and got mad. Sometimes he said things that made me cry and when I could not take it anymore, I ran into the bathroom, locked the door, and stayed inside until I stopped crying.

One year after my retirement, I did some soul-searching. My solo flight on the journey of my life at this juncture was on autopilot. I felt numb towards Madison. I carried out my daily chores without giving any thoughts to what I was doing. This was not the way to spend my retirement. I would stop crying no matter what Madison said. I did not find any love at home, but I realized that love did not have to be confined in one's living room or bedroom. I would give love to anyone I could give it to. I loved Leonard with all my heart and I knew he felt it.

Chinese New Year 2003 was on February 1st, the year of the lamb. Early that day the space shuttle with an Israeli astronaut on board broke apart on re-entry into the earth's atmosphere over Texas, U.S.

In March the U.S. was at war with Iraq. Around the same time, SARS first surfaced in China and then spread to other parts of the world. An old Chinese lady went from Toronto to Hong Kong. She stayed in the same hotel as a man from China who had SARS. When she came back to Toronto she was diagnosed with the same disease and died eventually. This was a novel virus and it had not been around for long so not a lot was known about it. The Canadian health officials were not prepared for it. Toronto was hit the hardest. The largest ethnic groups were found there. A lot of people liked to go there either to live or visit. They said Toronto was the centre of the universe and that SARS was one flight away. Many Torontonians were infected and some succumbed to it. We stayed home most of the time. The epidemic slowly died down after several months. The death toll was forty-four in Canada.

Jane and her two daughters were in Toronto in July. On August 14th, Olivia drove us all to Stratford, Ontario, to watch a play called "Hunchback of Notre Dame." On our way out of the theatre after the show, the electricity went off. We began our trip back to Toronto. All the traffic lights in Stratford were not working. Halfway home, Olivia got a call on her cell phone from George telling her that there was a blackout in Ontario and part of the U.S. It started in Ohio and eight of the states in America were affected. Millions of people were without power. The next day most offices and banks were closed. We got the power back on in the afternoon.

A lot of commotions occurred in 2003. When life was finally back to normal in the latter part of that year, I took the train to Vancouver to see my uncles and aunts. I boarded the train in Toronto early one morning at the beginning of November. Unlike my trip on the train from Vancouver to Toronto in 1968, this was a leisurely ride. I paid the fare for the economy class. Since it was the low season, I could take up the empty seat beside me so I could lie down to sleep at night.

The scenery along the route was beautiful, especially when I got near Edmonton where I saw the Rocky Mountains which were magnificent, majestic, and breathtaking. There were deer and elk perching on the rugged rocky slopes of the mountains.

When the train was near the border of British Columbia, it made a left turn to its final destination, Vancouver. It travelled along a stream running through the forests. There was a full moon that night when we passed by Mount Robson, the tallest of the Rockies in Canada.

Early next morning, we arrived in Vancouver. My trip took three days and three nights. Aunt Betty was at the train station to pick me up. She asked me as soon as she saw me, "Do you want to take the Greyhound bus with me to Los Angeles to see Bradly and Merton?" Bradley and Merton were her two sons working in Los Angeles.

I replied, "I'd love to. I have never been there."

Without leaving the train station, we obtained the bus tickets since the Greyhound buses and the trains shared the same station. I stayed in Vancouver for a few days before the bus trip during which time I got together with Aunt May, Uncle Bill, Uncle Bob, and their families.

The Greyhound bus was scheduled to leave Vancouver early in the morning and arrive in Los Angeles in the late afternoon the next day. We stayed with Merton and his wife, Tessa. Bradley, his wife, Eileen, and their son Cliff came over to see us.

Merton took us to all the beaches along the scenic Pacific coast. We went to the Kodak Theatre in Hollywood and Universal Studios. Merton also drove us to Las Vegas on the weekend. We went to the casinos and watched two shows at the hotels. After we got back from Las Vegas it was time for us to go back to Vancouver where I stayed with Uncle Bill and Aunt Susan until I took the train back to Toronto after I was away for one month.

The return train trip was so pleasant that the day before I arrived in Toronto I did not wish my trip to end so soon.

Once I was back home I kept quiet most of the time, since I realized that Madison did not like me to speak, so I zipped up my lips which made life more bearable. One time I could not help myself and talked back to him.

He said, "You are bitter."

I replied, "I've been called worse." That shut him up.

Corinne sometimes came to Toronto to visit her two sisters. We met whenever she was in town. One afternoon I told Madison that I would have dinner with Corinne.

He said, "Why are you telling me this now? Let me know as soon as you find out when you will go out."

I found that ridiculous. He just wanted badly to put a grip on me.

I replied, "Next time when I know when I will go out, I will tell you at the time I leave or I may not tell you that I am going out at all."

He said, "I chose the wrong woman to be my wife."

I became defiant and said, "I chose the wrong man to be my husband." We were not on the same wavelength.

I should have accepted the proposal from an angel instead of from a demon.

At the end of 2003, on the advice of his best friend, Tyler, David bought a one-bedroom plus a den condominium apartment unit. He was convinced by Tyler that it was fine for him to pay rent as long as he was working, but when he retired, a big portion of his monthly pension would go to the rent payment and he might have difficulty making ends meet. I gave him the $10,000 Mommy wanted me to hold onto for him.

In early 2004, I noticed that the gap between my right front tooth and the tooth right beside it closed by itself. My buckteeth was not so obvious anymore.

In the summer of 2004, Olivia drove Irene and me to New York City. We stayed in a hotel near Times Square. We took the subway to Ground Zero and from there walked across the Brooklyn Bridge and went back to our hotel on the subway. We saw the Broadway show "Rent" while in New York.

On Boxing Day 2004, there was a tsunami that originated in Indonesia and swept through Sri Lanka, Phuket Island, Malaysia, and stretched as far away as Africa. Around 230,000 lives, most of them Indonesian and some tourists from other parts of the world, were washed away into the ocean.

Jane's oldest daughter, Elizabeth, left Hong Kong and came back to study at a university in Montreal in 2005. She stayed with Mommy for several weeks before school started. One day she went out and would come back at dinnertime. David came to see Mommy that afternoon and before he left Elizabeth returned early. They met again after all these years.

One day I went to see Mommy, Emma was there too. She and Elizabeth were having a conversation on being lesbian and sounded like they might become one. I was alarmed.

I phoned David and mentioned to him what Emma and Elizabeth had said. I told him not to tell them he was gay.

He replied, "You hurt my feelings."

I said, "I am sorry."

I had his best interest at heart. I did not want my effort to bring him back to the fold in vain.

That summer I went to Vancouver, British Columbia, again. That time I flew. I stayed with Aunt Betty for a few days and then went to visit Madison's fifth sister, Bertha, her husband, Kent, and their family in Calgary. They drove me to the Banff National Park and Lake Louise, named after Queen Victoria's daughter, Princess Louise. We passed by the Rockies and I watched them up close, which made them look more spectacular. We went up to the peak of one of the mountains in a gondola. It was an awesome experience. They also took me to Drumheller where the dinosaurs once roamed.

Near the end of my stay in Calgary, Bertha said to me, "I have asked Madison to come to Calgary twenty times already. I asked him again this year and he said he would come next year."

Knowing him I was certain it would never materialize. I said, "If he comes next year, I will come again with him."

Kent said immediately, "Smart girl."

After I got back from Vancouver, I went to Ottawa. One night I had dinner with Corinne and Bryna at an Italian restaurant. During dinner, an Air France plane veered off course after touching down at the Toronto Pearson Airport. It was engulfed in flames. Luckily everybody on board evacuated from the burning plane within a matter of minutes. There was no fatality. Ever since then, the three of us stopped eating out together for fear of recurring aviation mishaps whenever we met this way.

One day in the summer of 2006, I went to see Mommy. She looked distraught and relayed to me what David had said to her, "Your worst fear has come true," implying that he had contracted either HIV or AIDS.

I could not bear to see Mommy being so devastated. I comforted her and said, "It is your own health you have to think of. Don't worry about anything."

I could not do the same myself. I was dealt a severe blow and had not felt so much grief before. It felt like my heart had been pierced and blood kept on flowing down. I did not want my brother's life to end tragically. I knew he had friends who were gay, but he did not have any partner.

After a short time I thought of cousin Rose in Vancouver. She was close to David. I sought her help to find out exactly what was going on with David. She agreed to look into it.

At the end of November Uncle Harold died. David went to Vancouver for the funeral.

A few weeks later Rose phoned me. She said, "After Uncle Harold's funeral, I made arrangements for David to have lunch with his daughter, cousin Gail, who is a very good communicator. David told her that what he said to Mommy was his way to get back at us who treated him poorly. He said he wanted to stay healthy and live to be one hundred."

Mommy and I were much relieved to learn the truth. David resumed seeing Mommy who welcomed him back.

By 2006, I began to find activities outside my home. I went line dancing once a week. After the dance, four or five of us in the same class went for coffee. We also played mah-jong twice a week at one of their houses.

After line dancing class one afternoon, one of my friends told me that instead of going to her house to play mah-jong the next day we would play at her friend's house. Her friend, Mrs. Au, bought a new solid-wood mah-jong table and she wanted to try it out with her. A while after we started the game, Mrs. Au's husband appeared and talked to us. He mentioned that he was the owner of a Chinese restaurant in Toronto. If a customer at his restaurant ordered a one-and-a-half-pound lobster, he would not give his customer one that weighed less and charged the full price.

I asked him, "What was the name of your restaurant?"

He replied, "Peking Palace."

I was surprised when I heard that and I said, "That was where my husband and I went to have nice Chinese food and we had our wedding reception there in 1969."

He said, "This was where the parents of one of my daughters-in-law had their wedding reception too."

He told us that he went from Hong Kong to Taiwan to attend university. He graduated with a bachelor degree in agriculture. He came to Canada in the early 1960s.

When we ate there in the 1960s I saw him at the reception area. After forty-some years, I had the chance to see him again in his house and to know him a bit more.

Although I paid the loan for our family car, Madison did not want me to use it. I had to ask him to drive me whenever I needed to. He did not like to give me the ride the same day I requested it. He told me to give him at least twenty-four-hours' notice. I found that unreasonable so I decided to take public transit instead.

I had not cried for a long time, but in 2007 or 2008 at one of the American Idol shows on television, Josh Groban made a guest appearance singing "You Raise Me Up." A choir made up of a large group of African children performed with him. A young girl with her front teeth missing stood in the front row. She reminded me of my black teeth when I was small. I felt pity for her but I did not cry.

The following afternoon I saw the same choir performance repeated on "The Ellen DeGeneres Show." She remarked that watching those African children sing made her cry. On hearing this, I cried too as she wiped away her tears.

On Valentine's Day 2008, Uncle Bill phoned me from Vancouver. He told me the night before Uncle Bob drove to meet his friends for dinner. He suffered a heart attack on his way. He lost control of his car and was unconscious. The paramedic failed to revive him. He was seventy-three years old.

In May, Corinne's older sister, Sylvia, and her husband, Darcy, wanted to visit London, England. I teamed up with them so I could see Mr. Harrison who retired in 1989 and was residing in Bournemouth right by the English Channel. We stayed in a hotel near the Tower of London.

I phoned Mr. Harrison the afternoon I arrived in London. He instructed me to take the train at the Waterloo train station to go to Bournemouth the next day. Early the following morning, I went on the underground to get to the train station. The train ride took two hours. I was thrilled to see Mr. Harrison and his wife, Alexi. We had lunch at a restaurant in a seaside hotel.

After lunch I went to their apartment. Since I had not seen Mr. Harrison for thirty-seven years, we had a lot of catching up to do. It was a memorable reunion.

The next day Sylvia, Darcy, and I went to tour the Tower of London. A tour guide dressed in a beefeater costume told us about the persons imprisoned in the tower. One of them was Anne Boleyn who was led from the tower up to Tower Hill to be beheaded. He also told us a story about a more than six-foot-tall Scotsman being locked up in the tower. Every day his wife visited him with several of her lady friends. After the wife's visit one day, the cell where the Scotsman stayed was empty. While the wife was there to see him, he dressed up as a lady and left the tower with the women. The tour guide asked us what that was called. I knew the answer but I did not know the story behind it. That was how *scot-free* originated. He was a very entertaining guide. I gave him a big tip.

On the following two days, we went sightseeing in London. We were outside Buckingham Palace, 10 Downing Street, and

Westminster Abbey. We had dinner in Chinatown which is close to Trafalgar Square.

After a four-day stay in London, we flew from Gatwick airport to Florence, Italy. We were there for three days before we went to Venice where Corinne joined us to embark on a twelve-day Mediterranean cruise.

Our first stop was Dubrovnik. Our next stop was Katakolon where we saw the ancient Olympic City. We then went to Kusadasi, Turkey. From there we went to Athens and several Greek islands including Santorini. We stopped in Naples where we took the train to see the ruins in Pompeii.

We disembarked in Rome and stayed there for a few days. We visited Vatican City and toured the Sistine Chapel.

Our final stop was Paris. We were there for four days. We went to the Louvre to see Da Vinci's *Mona Lisa* behind the Plexiglas from a distance, also Notre Dame Cathedral, the Eiffel Tower, and Versailles.

When I arrived back in Toronto and went through immigration, the immigration officer asked me, "Where did you go?"

I replied, "London, Paris, and a Mediterranean cruise in between."

He said, "Wow!"

I loved my first cruise so much that in September that same year I went on a one-week New England cruise with friends I played mah-jong with. The ship sailed along the Atlantic coast of Canada and the U.S.A. We embarked and disembarked in New York City.

In May the following year, I took another cruise with Corinne. This time we went to Alaska for one week. I went to Vancouver a few days in advance in order to spend some time with Aunt Betty and Uncle Bill, since that was where we would embark on our cruise.

The day I flew back to Toronto, I saw the new double-decker Airbus A380 landed for the first time at the Toronto Pearson International Airport.

Soon after I came back from my trip, I started to volunteer at a long-term care home for four hours a week during the summer months. I felt a closeness with the old residents in this home, no doubt from all the years I had lived with ah mah and porh pawh.

One afternoon, I ate out with a Chinese couple I socialized with in Ottawa before they moved to Toronto in the 1980s. We resumed our gathering together periodically since we were back in the same city. In the 1950s when Neal, the husband, was four years old, he immigrated from Hong Kong to Alberta with his mother and two older brothers to join their father who came alone a few years earlier. Neal's father settled down in Vulcan made famous by the Star Trek series. He operated a laundromat there.

While we were having our lunch, Gene Pitney's song "Town Without Pity" was playing in the restaurant. Neal recalled that when he was a teenager in Vulcan, he listened to hit songs together with his friends who were at a distance through walkie-talkie.

That summer, Jane and Mark came to Toronto to be with Elizabeth and Rhoda who was attending the same university as her sister. They were staying with Mommy. One day, David phoned Mommy and Jane took the call. He asked her if he could come over to see Mommy and she said yes. They got reunited.

Around this time, we noticed Jane became absent-minded. She put her eyeglasses inside the medicine cabinet in the bathroom and forgot where she had put them. She had difficulties paying with cash. She even forgot her date of birth. She shrugged it off as a lapse of memory.

Back in Hong Kong one afternoon, she had a lunch date with a friend. She had problems finding her way to the restaurant. She got lost and started to panic. She phoned Mark to tell him to cancel her lunch date for her and to come to get her. She was diagnosed with Alzheimer's disease and had to be on medication. She was only in her early fifties. She could not do any housework. Mark hired a live-in maid to handle the chores. She still knew her way around her apartment building, so every morning she went out for a walk alone. When she ate she could not tell a fork from a knife. She lost her cognitive ability.

The World Exposition in 2010 took place in Shanghai, China. Sylvia, Corinne, and I planned on going. I told a couple of my good friends that I was running away from home temporarily. The logo on the chimney of one of the cruise ships is "Escape Completely." That was my way of making the great escape.

I went alone to Hong Kong after the Chinese New Year in February. After staying with Jane and Mark for one week, I flew to Sydney, Australia, to visit Paula who was a former classmate of mine and Catherine's. Catherine came from Brisbane to Sydney for a reunion with us. We joined a tour that took us inside the iconic Sydney Opera House. Early that morning, there was a photographer taking a photo of the backs of naked men and women on the steps of the opera house. The photo appeared in the local newspaper with the headline "Start Spreading the Nudes."

After a few days, Catherine went back to Brisbane with me. She suggested I should go to the Great Barrier Reef. We went to a travel agency and an agent put together a fantastic package for me. I would not give up a once-in-a-lifetime chance to witness the wonder of nature. It was a three days' stay in a hotel resort in Port Douglas. The return airfare, admission fees to the attractions, and two lunches were included. Transportation was provided everywhere I went in Port Douglas.

I was in a glass-bottom boat to view the coral reef and the sea creatures. I went to a crocodile farm where they raised crocodiles from birth till they were fully grown.

I came back from Port Douglas to Brisbane and stayed with Catherine for one more week before I flew back to Hong Kong.

Sylvia and Corinne arrived from Canada soon after and we began our trip to China.

Our first destination was Sian, the former capital of China. It was steeped in history, which dated back five-thousand-plus years. We went to see the terracotta soldiers and other historical sites.

Our next stop was Beijing, the present-day capital of China. We went to the Great Wall of China, Tiananmen Square, the Forbidden City, and the Summer Palace.

We arrived in Shanghai after one week in Beijing. We stayed in a hotel right by the Bund. Before we went to the exposition, we were on a seven-day cruise that took us to Japan and South Korea. Our ports of call were Kagoshima, Nagasaki, and Fukuoka in Japan, and Busan in South Korea.

We spent three days at the World Exposition. We visited the modern China. These big Chinese cities are the same as those all over the world.

At the end of our stay in Shanghai, I parted company with Sylvia and Corinne. I returned to Hong Kong and remained there till the middle of May. I was away for three months.

One month after I got back home, I received a letter from Mr. Harrison breaking the news that his wife, Alexi, died earlier in the year. She was in her eighties.

Jane and Mark were in Toronto in the summer. George arranged a family gathering at a restaurant. He told me to ask David to come along too. He said when he phoned Jane in Hong Kong earlier, David answered the phone. He was visiting her. George knew it was time for him to reunite with David. What seemed to be mission impossible at first had become mission accomplished after eighteen years.

At the end of that year, Heather found out she had ovarian cancer and underwent surgery. The tumour was removed.

In March 2011, Japan was struck by a strong earthquake that triggered a tsunami. It caused great devastation and debris could be found as far away as the west coast of the U.S.

Corinne and I had booked a vacation in Honolulu in two months' time. The tsunami might have hit Hawaii but luckily it did not. In May, we went on our trip as planned. We stayed in a hotel overlooking the Waikiki Beach where we watched people surfing.

At the end of that week, we embarked on a one-week Hawaiian cruise sailing from Honolulu to Maui, the Big Island, and Kauai.

Another dream had come true. When I stopped over in Honolulu on my way to Canada in 1967, I wished I could go back there one day. I found Hawaii a paradise on earth.

I had to face reality again once home. One day Olivia brought up the subject of the expensive funeral cost.

She said, "Mommy does not have a lot of savings. When she dies, you children will have to come up with a hefty sum of money to foot the bill."

I had the power of attorney for Mommy's bank account. I knew exactly how much money she had. It would be enough to cover the expenses involved. It was a chequing account which did not pay interest. I suggested to her to invest half the amount in a term deposit which paid some interest. She did not like the idea and thought I was after her money. I was in her bad book. She did not include me in any family gatherings for months.

When Jane and Mark were in Toronto in the summer, she expressed her intention of moving out of their apartment because she did not want to die in other people's homes.

Mark took her to look for rental apartments and found one. It was a unit with two bedrooms and two bathrooms. The rent was $2,000 monthly. Mommy needed all the money she had to pay the rent.

Mark arranged and paid for a young Chinese cleaning lady, Vera, to do the housecleaning for Mommy once a week. I was in charge of paying Vera once a month.

Early in 2012, I planned another trip with Sylvia and Corinne. It was a two-week China and Southeast Asia cruise. Afterwards I would spend four weeks with Jane in Hong Kong.

One week before my trip, Vera phoned me and said while crying, "Your mother said I was not doing a good job. She treated me badly. I want to quit."

I said, "My mother is an old lady. You know how some old people like things done their own way. Please bear with her and help her out."

I then made a call to Mommy and told her what Vera had said on the phone.

It was Mommy's turn to cry while saying, "I had hired three maids when you were small and I had no problem with any of them. I don't like the way she handles the cleaning."

I replied, "I will be going away next week for one and a half months. I can't settle things for you till I come back. If the two of you can't wait that long, let's see who will be the first to let the other one go."

We went to Beijing again for a few days in mid-February. We went up to the Great Wall of China for the second time. We left Beijing by bus that took us to Tianjin to embark on the cruise. We stopped at Nagasaki, Busan, Nha Tran, and Ho Chi Minh City. In Ho Chi Minh City, we had pho in a restaurant called Pho 2001, so named after Bill and Chelsea Clinton ate there in 2001. I followed Bill Clinton's footsteps again and went where he had gone before. There was a photo of the two of them having pho in the restaurant.

From Vietnam we sailed to Hong Kong and Bangkok. We disembarked in Singapore where we stayed overnight. The next day Sylvia and Corinne went back to Canada. I flew to Hong Kong and stayed with Jane. Her condition was stable at that time with the drug cocktail she was on. She could not carry on a conversation any more. All her friends had deserted her.

I left Hong Kong at the end of March right before I had a bad cold. I phoned Mommy when I got back home. She said she fired Vera three weeks after I left for my trip. She also said since she moved she had not received any mail, even though David and Olivia had made the necessary address changes for her.

She got government cheques for needy senior citizens in the mail periodically. She relied on these funds to supplement her monthly expenses. I told her I had to wait until I was well enough to help her. My cold did not get better and I had a persistent cough. Madison was disturbed by my coughing at night. He moved to the other room. I had the whole bed in the big bedroom all to myself.

I recovered in the middle of May. I checked with David and Olivia to find out where they sent Mommy's address changes to.

Olivia said, "I contacted the Canadian Government Service Centre. If there is any problem, somebody has to take care of it."

I did not intend to ask her to look after it. All I wanted was to know where to go to follow it up. The officer at the Government Service Centre gave me instructions on how to proceed. I called the appropriate government department and fixed the problem.

Mommy appreciated what I had done for her. She finally saw the light and said to me, "Fong Ting, you are the one who can make things right."

Up until then she did not think too highly of me. I felt that was the moment to reconcile with her and remove the barricade between us. Silently, I declared a truce with her. I would not be the rebellious daughter I once was. I would be there for her to give her hope in her twilight years.

She went out more to shop and dine with me. After a few months I found she had trouble following instructions. She showed signs of dementia. In the fall, her health deteriorated. She had high white blood cell counts. Both her kidneys did not function well.

She was in and out of the hospital a few times and at the end of 2012 she moved to a long-term care home.

Madison found out he had high cholesterol and high blood pressure at his yearly physical checkup that year. He told his family doctor that his high blood pressure was caused by the stress from me, when in fact it was the other way around. His doctor suggested he and I should seek help from marriage counselling. He did not really want to go, but if he did, I would not go with him. I knew he was beyond help.

He could no longer stand the silent treatment from me. There was hidden writing on the wall not for me to see. He voiced his dismay to his number eight sister in Toronto, his older brother's daughter, his favourite niece, Trudy, also in Toronto and a few of his friends behind my back. The news travelled far and wide. One night I was home with him and the phone rang. He answered it and the call was from Los Angeles. The first thing he said was he was alone by himself. As he carried on the conversation, I gathered the call was from Trudy's uncle who was the younger brother of her mother in Vancouver. She told him about Madison's disgruntlement. Shortly after, the wife of one of Madison's friends in Ottawa called me and warned me that Madison was considering a divorce, and I sensed that he must be serious this time. I hunkered down in anticipation of having to face the inevitable, and would await his move.

Soon after New Year 2013, Madison had severe backaches. He went for an X-ray, which showed the discs in his spine started to degenerate.

In early February, Mommy's health became worse. She was hospitalized till the end of the month when she died. She was eighty-nine years old. Right after Papa died, I hoped Mommy would have a long life because she was the only parent I had.

In May, I went to Bournemouth to see Mr. Harrison again for one week. He invited me to stay with him. I accepted his invitation.

He had said before that if I went to see him again, he would show me his part of the country and that was what he did. It was a picturesque part of the country. We had lunch at a restaurant by the English Channel across from the Isle of Wight where Queen Victoria's summer palace was. One afternoon we had dim sum at a Chinese restaurant in Bournemouth.

Before we went out for lunch one morning, we sat down and chatted. Mr. Harrison asked, "Why did you move to Toronto instead of settling down in Vancouver?"

I told him the reason behind my decision.

He said, "You're a pioneer woman." He asked again, "Have you ever considered going back to Hong Kong?"

I replied, "That Andrew Smith guy asked if I wanted to go with him to work in Hong Kong."

He did not pursue any further for he had no doubt known what ensued.

On the last day of my stay, Mr. Harrison drove me to Dorset which was west of Bournemouth. We had lunch at a restaurant overlooking a lovely beach in West Bay where the Jurassic Coast is. On the way back, Mr. Harrison took the scenic route. We passed by beaches sprawling along the coast of the English Channel, and some traditional English cottages by the side of the highway.

When we got back to Mr. Harrison's home that evening, I said to him, "I did not recall what the movie *Far from the Madding Crowd* was about. I saw it in the early 1970s, but I clearly remembered the scene when Julie Christie was by the beach, which looked like the one in West Bay."

He replied, "That was where the story took place. The author, Thomas Hardy, was from Dorset."

He told me about the Dorset apple cake, which I found at the food court in Heathrow Airport. It was delicious and different from any apple cakes I had in Canada.

Two months after I came back from England, Corinne and I went to Halifax, Peggy's Cove, and St. John's, which I liked to return to.

On my return to Toronto, Leonard told me about his engagement to Larissa, a lady he met several years ago. She was born in Canada of Japanese descent. The wedding would take place in one year's time.

Meanwhile, Madison experienced pain in his hip and legs too. He went for a CAT scan that showed he had bone cancer. He had to go to the hospital immediately and stayed behind for radiation treatment. If his cancer was not treated quickly, he would be crippled.

The oncologist found out his cancer originated in his lung and spread to his liver and bones. The tumour in his bone was gone after radiation. At the end of his two weeks' stay in the hospital, he came back home. He went on chemotherapy for the cancer in his lung and liver.

A few days before Christmas, we were hit by an ice storm in Toronto. It was déjà vu. I thought the ice storm in 1998 would happen only once in my life. I had to live through another one that lasted for a few days.

We had a very quiet Christmas and New Year. Madison was in no condition to celebrate. He suffered side effects from the chemotherapy. He woke up a few times at night. One day he said to me, "I should not stay up so late all these years. I needed more rest to be healthy."

Leonard and Larissa would get married in the beginning of August 2014. They began to look for a house they could move into after the wedding. Leonard put his apartment up for sale. His dog, Lotus, moved in with me. Leonard and Larissa found a house in midtown soon after he sold his apartment. Lotus stayed behind with me because Leonard was busy with preparing for the wedding and packing for the move.

One Sunday, Leonard came over to spend some time with Lotus. He mentioned that one side of his ears was blocked and he had a bleeding nose sometimes. His family physician, Dr. Chan, who was the son-in-law of Madison's number nine sister, the one who bullied him the most. Dr. Chan's diagnosis was that it was allergies and told Leonard to take an antihistamine. I warned him to pay attention to its progress because a bleeding nose might be a sign of cancer.

In May, Madison's oncologist, Dr. Finch, sent him for an MRI that showed the tumour in his lung and liver had shrunk somewhat, but cancerous cells were detected in his brain. He had to undergo radiation on the brain tumour. After a few radiation treatments, his body began to shake involuntarily. He thought he had Parkinson's disease. In the second week of July, he complained the food he had for breakfast that morning did not taste good and the piece of pizza for lunch was lousy.

I took Lotus out for a walk that afternoon. When I returned home after fifteen minutes I found Madison lying on the floor unconscious. I called 911 immediately. An ambulance came to take him to hospital. I went along with him. It was the first time I was in an ambulance with the siren on. The doctor who was on duty in the emergency room said he suffered a seizure. The nurse said that he was in a grave condition and someone should be with me. I called Leonard and when I got hold of him I asked him where he was. He said, "Larissa and I are on our way to the travel agency to book a trip to Paris on our honeymoon."

He and Larissa came to the hospital after they sent Madison for a CAT scan. The doctor found from the scan that his brain tumour did not respond to the treatment. He had to be admitted to the hospital.

Leonard and Larissa left the hospital to go to take care of Lotus. I waited until Madison had settled in his room before I went home.

I went back to the hospital the next day. The nurse said I needed to spend the night with Madison in the hospital because he tried to get out of bed all night and he might fall. He was in a private room where there was a bedsitting chair I could sleep on. He tried to get out of bed in the middle of the night to go to the bathroom even though he was hooked up to a catheter. There were guardrails on the sides of the bed, but one night he managed to slide down to the foot of the bed where the rail did not reach that far. I woke up just in time, but I was not able to restrain him. I rang the nurse for help. She said I had to stay up all night to keep an eye on him.

One evening, a patient named Mr. Wang in a room nearby had many visitors. He was moaning and groaning and it appeared that he was in critical condition. I was woken up in the middle of the night when I heard a lot of commotion as Mr. Wang was being transferred to somewhere else. I got up and looked out the hallway and saw someone standing at the open door in the dark. I was so scared when I thought that it was Madison who had managed to make his way to the door. The person then spoke. It was the nurse who came to check on Madison.

The following day Madison was moved to a general ward with three other patients. One of them was an older Chinese man from Trinidad. There was another older man from Naples, Italy, who refused to change into the hospital gown. He told me he immigrated to Canada in 1966. The third patient was a middle-aged man from Russia. He said he knew karate.

There was no bedsitting chair in the general ward. At night, I put two armchairs together, one facing the other, but it was not the length of a bed. When I lay down, I dangled my feet over one of its sides. All four patients snored loudly at night. I was a sound sleeper so it did not bother me.

One morning the Italian old man said to me, "You are nice. You stayed with your brother at night in the hospital."

I replied, "He is not my brother. He is my husband."

144

I slept in the hospital for nine nights. Finally, Madison stopped his attempt to get out of bed. Dr. Finch did not know why Madison wanted to get out of bed until I told him he wanted to go to the bathroom.

At the end of his two weeks' stay in the hospital, Dr. Finch sent him for an MRI that showed his brain cancer was incurable. Dr. Finch said to him, "You have less than three months to live. You will go to a hospice to die." Madison was handed his death sentence.

Three days before Leonard and Larissa's wedding, Madison was transferred to a hospice. He wanted to attend the wedding ceremony. He was confined in a wheelchair so I had to make arrangements for special transportation for him to get around.

Two days before the wedding Leonard came to see me. He told me that one side of his neck was swollen. I told Leonard I would make an appointment for him with Dr. Stokowski who shared the office with my family doctor, Dr. Goldman.

It was a beautiful sunny Saturday afternoon in the summer when Leonard and Larissa exchanged wedding vows in an outdoor ceremony. Madison had a beer and a bite to eat before I dropped him back to the hospice.

Dr. Stokowski sent Leonard for a scan that showed he had cancer and was referred to Dr. Orr at a cancer hospital which is one of the top five cancer research centres in the world. According to the scan, Leonard had a rare form of cancer which was in his nose and neck. At that time there were only seventy-five to one hundred people among the entire world's population who had this type of cancer.

We did not want Madison to know that his son also had cancer when he was about to die from it. We did not mention this to his sisters either.

Madison had been at the hospice for three weeks when his doctor, Dr. Cohen, phoned me.

She said, "This morning I asked Madison to raise his left hand and foot but he was not able to although he said he could. The only way to find out is from a scan. There is no scanner here. We have to send him to a hospital. He may have to stay there for a few days and when he is released there may not be a bed available for him here."

I replied, "Dr. Finch said Madison was to go to the hospice to die. I don't think it is necessary to know what the cause is."

He was given sedatives and slept most of the time. He could eat only blended food. In the beginning of the fourth week of September, Dr. Cohen phoned me and said, "Madison will die sometime this week."

Late at night in the middle of that week, the nurse at the hospice called me and said, "Your husband's condition has worsened. You may want to come over to be with him."

Before I left home, I phoned Leonard to relay the news to him.

He said, "I have to go for a PET scan at 7:30 a.m. tomorrow. I will not go to the hospice with you."

Lotus was still staying with me.

I said to Leonard, "If I have to stay in the hospice until late tomorrow morning, I won't be able to tend to Lotus."

Leonard replied, "There's nothing I can do."

I had to go to the hospice immediately and would deal with this matter when the morning came. I took a taxi there. When the nurse saw me, he told me Madison might hang in there all through the night. I sat on a chair beside his bed and fell asleep. When I woke up at 2:15 a.m. I found Madison had stopped breathing. The nurse examined him and pronounced he had died.

Madison died soon after our forty-fifth wedding anniversary. Our loveless and tumultuous marriage finally came to an end. Living with Madison was worse than living with Mommy. I jumped from the frying pan into the fire. I lived in a toxic environment. I had a close, lengthy, and agonizing encounter with Madison, the

MAD MAN. All the wrongs his sisters had done to him, he took them out on me. Leonard bore some of the brunt.

It would have been Madison's seventy-second birthday on the day of his funeral. Leonard concluded his eulogy by saying that he had to battle his own cancer.

One week before Thanksgiving, Leonard started his cancer treatment, which was for seven weeks. He underwent radiation once a week with a few overnight chemotherapy treatments in between. Dr. Orr told him that after two or three weeks of radiation, the swelling in his neck would go away.

By the time the swelling in Leonard's neck disappeared, he was drained physically and mentally. He said to me, "November is going to be a long month."

I replied, "You said in your eulogy to your dad that you had to battle your own cancer. Battle is hard. You have to fight with all your might."

The ordeal for Leonard was finally over at the end of November and he bounced back shortly. We all had Christmas dinner at the house of Larissa's oldest sister.

On their first wedding anniversary, Leonard and Larissa went to Paris where they were supposed to go for their honeymoon. Leonard went back to work when he returned from Paris. Larissa was supposed to be at work that same day but she did not feel well. She went to the hospital and had some tests and scans that showed she had cervical cancer. She had chemotherapy and radiation treatment at the same cancer hospital Leonard went to. Her tumour was gone after six months. They began their married life on the wrong foot with both of them stricken with life-threatening diseases.

I had a part-time job as a dog walker. From Monday to Friday when Leonard and Larissa were at work, I went over to their house in the afternoon to take Lotus and Jackie, Larissa's bulldog, to the park nearby.

Larissa has an older sister who is married with two grown-up children. She also has a younger sister who is married with no children. Her brother is the youngest in the family and he is single. Their mother lives alone in a house just north of Toronto.

Larissa is very thoughtful and considerate. She said since I am by myself, she invites me to join in celebrating special occasions and festivities with her family.

Soon after Easter in 2018, freezing rain fell incessantly on the weekend. We were advised not to go out if it was not necessary. I skipped Sunday mass. When I finally went out at the beginning of the week, the sidewalks were encrusted with ice. It was cold and dreary.

It was a completely different picture one week later, which was Monday, April 23rd. We woke up to a beautiful, sunny spring day. The ice on the sidewalks had all melted. It brought people out in droves. I had to go to the bank nearby that afternoon. By the time I left home, I found more pedestrians than normal and the traffic was heavier in front of my apartment building. As I walked further down towards Yonge Street, which is one block west of the street I am on and the longest street in the world, I saw both sides of the street were cordoned off by yellow tapes and many policemen were standing guard. I turned and went back home. I was shocked when I heard on the news that an hour earlier a man in his twenties in a rented white van mowed down the sidewalks along Yonge Street. Two men and eight women, some young and some old, died at the scene. Sixteen people were injured, some critically.

One of the dead women in her early thirties used to work in the same company as Leonard. They played games occasionally at lunchtime.

The driver stopped the van several blocks away. He got out and stood on the sidewalk. A Chinese policeman, a former engineer, de-escalated the crisis. He reached inside the patrol car and shut off the siren. He executed a calm takedown without firing a single gunshot. He handcuffed the attacker who was lying on the ground. The whole incident was captured on video and appeared on the headlines of newspapers in other parts of the world.

Similar attacks had been carried out in cities in other countries. Toronto was not immune, but it was inconceivable that it had taken place almost right at my doorstep.

On my way to the bank the next morning, I saw a worker from a graffiti removal company spraying away the bloodstain on the sidewalk. There were vans from all the major television stations, including those from the U.S., spotted on the nearby side streets.

Traffic was not allowed in that stretch of the street for a few days. The police investigation concluded that it was not terrorism. The accused man was later found guilty of ten counts of murder and sixteen counts of attempted murder.

At the end of 2019, thousands of citizens in Wuhan, China, were infected with a novel coronavirus. In January 2020, the first case of that virus was detected in Canada. Early in 2020, this virus had spread to most parts of the world.

Just as I thought I had been through everything, life threw me a once-in-a-century pandemic that was declared by the World Health Organization in March 2020, and named the disease COVID-19.

I had to grapple with this highly infectious disease. There were variant after variant, wave after wave, and lockdown after lockdown. I was in self-isolation. I went out only if absolutely necessary with face masks on. I did not dare to be outdoors for too long. I felt like I was living in wartime.

We had to practise physical distancing and wash our hands frequently. I could not see Leonard, Larissa, and her family for several months. All we could do was to gather every weekend at Zoom meetings.

Vaccines were developed near the end of 2020. Normally it would take several years.

The life of the concubine's granddaughter is a dog's life, as fittingly, I was born in the year of the dog. It may very well be that of a cat that has nine lives. Like a cat, I feel that I have lived through many lives-none of them sheltered. I've never had it easy, but then, I am not one to take the easy way out and I do not give up too easily. Actually I have had more than my fair share of living, and what I have been through is not for the faint of heart. I am one of those who thrive in adverse conditions; it is then I unleash my built-in strength.

My solo long-haul flight in life is fraught with turbulence, but I have come out of it unscathed, my sanity intact, I have reached my full potential and found inner peace.

Sir Edmund Hillary said, "It was not the mountain that we conquered but ourselves."

I always remind myself of the song that goes, "Accentuate the positive. Eliminate the negative. Latch on to the affirmative."

An Ottawa newspaper once wrote about Matthew Perry in "Friends," another former Ottawan, quoting part of James Taylor's song that goes, "Life is a journey. Enjoy the passage of time."

All the things that have been said about dogs are not nice or pleasant except one that is: EVERY DOG HAS ITS DAY.

Nowadays even the underdog has its day!